LEGAL PRACTI(

NEGOTIATING
SKILLS

LEGAL PRACTICE HANDBOOK

NEGOTIATING SKILLS

Ann Halpern

Director, Legal Education and Training
Rowe & Maw, London

Series Editor: Anthony G. King, MA, Solicitor
Director of Education, Clifford Chance

BLACKSTONE
PRESS LIMITED

First published in Great Britain 1992 by Blackstone Press Limited,
9-15 Aldine Street, London W12 8AW. Telephone 081-740 1173

ISBN: 1 85431 170 0

British Library Cataloguing in Publication Data
A CIP catalogue record for this book is available from the British
Library

Typeset by Murdoch Evans Partnership, Tonbridge, Kent
Printed by BPCC Wheatons Ltd, Exeter

12   Preparation   **92**
12.1 Knowing the file   12.2 Knowing the law   12.3 Understanding
your client's instructions and objectives   12.4 Knowing the other
side's case and objectives   12.5 Knowing the other side   12.6
Expanding the cake   12.7 Preparing yourself   12.8 Preparing the
agenda and for the meeting   12.9 Summary   12.10 Preparation
checklists   12.10.1 The file and client information   12.10.2 Your
personal style, strategy and tactics

Bibliography   **108**

To RL who succumbed to my negotiating skills in agreeing to take over total responsibility for everything while I wrote, and to J who suffered stoically much shortened walks.

Preface

This book is designed primarily for those who are in the early stages of their careers in practice. Negotiating is one of the most important aspects of the work of any lawyer. You will not be able to exist in our practical legal world without at some time or another having to undertake a negotiation. *Negotiating Skills* is intended to help you make the transition from theory to practice, hopefully without making too many mistakes at the expense of your clients. Everybody negotiates — there is no other way to live in our world. But when others are paying you to act as their knight — to represent and protect their interests, to fight their corner, to get the best possible result for them — for you the experience can be extremely fraught. The more you understand about the whole process of negotiating the better you will be able to use the opportunities whilst still in training and in the early years post qualification to observe critically the behaviour and skills of others. You will benefit most when you are able to sit back and observe if you prepare as though you were taking overall responsibility for the negotiation. You will then be able to compare your approach with that taken by the fee earner you are watching. Where there are differences, use whatever opportunities there are to explore with the fee earner concerned why he or she approached the negotiation in the way that she or he chose. Try using your listening skills, for example 'I noticed that you chose to use a collaborative strategy when approaching this negotiation — how did you know that it would be effective, what preparation did you do, had you identified any risks in using this strategy, what would you have done if the other side had adopted a competitive strategy? . . .' and so on. Question and compare with your own approach what you see going on about you as often as you can.

When you are responsible for the conduct of a negotiation or a part of a negotiation constantly keep under review your own performance in a similar way. If you appraise your own performance and reflect on why you approached a negotiation in a particular way and how you carried it out the more you will be likely to enhance your skills. However difficult you may find asking for feedback or criticism, you will gain insights into your performance if you seek the views of your colleagues both before and after a negotiation.

The desire to understand the process of negotiation is not new and the recognition of its importance to legal practice has grown dramatically over the last few years. In particular it is now recognised in the vocational training courses for both branches of the profession. My interest in negotiating has grown from the time when I was in pupillage, through the development of the new vocational course for student barristers and now, in the highly-tuned world of commercial practice in the City. Many of the ideas in this book have crystallised as a result of the training programmes I have directed here at Rowe & Maw and from the discussions I have had with our partners, to whom I am indebted. The series editor, Tony King's comments and suggestions on an early draft were of invaluable help. In the final analysis however, any omissions, errors, inaccuracies or deficiencies are my own responsibility.

Ann Halpern
Rowe & Maw
London EC4
October 1992

Chapter One

Introduction

This book aims to help you understand and develop the particular qualities and skills required to become successful at negotiating in a legal context. Lawyers, whether in private practice or employed as in-house counsel, need to be able to negotiate as effectively as possible. For many, negotiating will be a major part of their day to day work. Commercial and property lawyers have always spent a great deal of their professional lives negotiating; today litigation lawyers also have to recognise how important effective negotiating skills are to them. The idea that lawyers spend most of their time taking their client's problems to court for resolution is long dead: something in the order of 90% of civil cases and around 99% of personal injury cases settle without getting into court. There is plenty of evidence to suggest that being an effective and skilful negotiator can radically influence the outcome of a matter and hence the overall advantage that your client obtains through the negotiating process. So being an effective negotiator means that you are able to perform a significant part of your professional duties well.

We are said to learn to negotiate even faster than we learn to speak; babies very quickly learn how to get what they want by crying! Some of us may continue to rely on this tactic, if we have found it to be effective, well into adulthood. Most of us though, as we grow older and become more sophisticated, will learn how to use a wide range of tactics and strategies to help us to get what we want, whether for ourselves or for our clients.

Effective negotiating skills can also be useful in many different day to day situations not exclusively related to the direct needs of your clients. In the context of the legal office, each and every time we carry out a task for someone, be it a client, a partner, another fee earner or the Director of Education and Training, we are entering a process of negotiating. We will seek to negotiate about such issues as when the work is required, how detailed an answer is wanted, what priority is to be given to this new task and where it ranks in the range of other things we are asked to do, how urgent the work is and so whether it should be completed before or after lunch, today or tomorrow. Equally each time we want a letter typed, an appointment made or someone to do our photocopying or filing, we will be negotiating. The styles, strategies and tactics described in this book are just as relevant in the context of the law office as they are when we negotiate on behalf of a client.

There is a wealth of literature about negotiating. Some authors concentrate on the international arena and the lessons to be learnt from the success or otherwise of the negotiation of peace treaties and disarmament accords. Others highlight the process of negotiating in the context of the business environment and the employment context, or seek to explain the process in psychological terms. This book relates that which is already well known in these other contexts to the legal field, seeking to transfer knowledge and identifiable skills wherever possible.

When seeking to develop any skill, written materials can only prepare the ground for practice. This book is intended to help both those who are just beginning to develop their skills in this field as well as those who already have experience in the professional context of negotiating. For those who have just begun their training, this book helps to analyse and explain the process of negotiating which trainees and pupils will see when shadowing their principal or pupilmaster. For those with experience, this book provides a framework for analysing and reviewing the skills gained through that experience and for developing and practising new ones. Whenever and wherever you negotiate, the aim is for you to feel satisfied that you have used your knowledge and skills so that you have achieved the best possible results for your clients, thereby enhancing your reputation and that of your firm, chambers or employer.

1.1 NEGOTIATION DEFINED

Lawyers seem to be particularly fond of definitions, so here is a selection of the many definitions which have been given to negotiation.

Negotiation is:

a basic means of getting what you want from others. It is back and forth communication designed to reach an agreement when you and the other side have some interests that are shared and others that are opposed;

a process of joint decision making used to handle issues as they arise in a particular social context;

communication for the purpose of persuasion;

a problem solving process in which two or more people voluntarily discuss their differences and attempt to reach a joint decision on their common concerns; and

an exchange of concessions or a quid pro quo — a willingness to enter into a form of give and take.

Each of these definitions has in common the idea that the parties should be willing to change their positions as a consequence of discussion and persuasion, and that usually this involves some exchange of concessions, until agreement is finally reached. For most psychologists, negotiation is seen as a game of strategy.

Having defined negotiation, it is also important to establish what makes a negotiation appear successful. A successful negotiation:

is one which satisfies the parties' competing interests as well as possible and as quickly as possible in ways that are seen to make sense so that the settlement is viable and sticks when put into effect (Hosking & Morley, *A Social Psychology of Organising: People, Processes and Contexts*).

1.2 THE LEGAL NEGOTIATION

1.2.1 The lawyer's quest for certainty

The lawyer's aim in most legal negotiations will be to negotiate until a legally enforceable agreement is reached. This means that the agreement reached must be clear, unambiguous and within the law so that it is legally capable of being enforced. An agreement which is legally enforceable is one through which the law will not run a coach and horses because, for example, it is contrary to competition law, or in some way illegal or contrary to public policy. In many commercial agreements consideration will need to be given to English law, foreign laws where there is a foreign element and to issues relating to jurisdiction and enforceability in a foreign jurisdiction.

Even so, occasionally ambiguity can be a very useful tool, especially when you are being put under pressure by a tight deadline and so are forced to leave some issues at least partly unresolved to help obtain the other side's agreement to the deal. Phrases like, 'best endeavours', 'reasonable endeavours', 'reasonable time', can help to save a negotiation and ensure that agreement is reached. However, if you fall back on any of these phrases, it is important to ensure that your client fully understands the potential risks in using them. The result could be fairly expensive if in the future the meaning of the agreement has to be litigated. Where ambiguous words or phrases are chosen they should never be so ambiguous that there is a risk that the whole agreement could fail for uncertainty. Agreements can fail even though courts will take a fairly purposive construction of a commercial agreement in order to give it effect, because they will not be prepared to rewrite the agreement for the parties.

1.2.2 Exposure to risk

A major aspect of your role in a legal negotiation will be to ensure that you minimise your client's exposure to future risk, whether financial or contractual.

Always ensure that you keep a good note of the negotiation meeting. It is to be hoped that there will never be a need to refer to your notes in the future, but if there were ever to be proceedings to rectify the contract, your notes could be invaluable.

1.3 MODES OF NEGOTIATING

This book mainly refers to the negotiations which are conducted face to face. However it is also possible for negotiations to be conducted by letter or by telephone. Which will be the most appropriate mode will often depend on the circumstances of the individual case. The mode you choose is really a tactical decision and there are advantages and disadvantages to each. These are dealt with in chapter 4.

1.4 ETHICAL ISSUES

The basic principle to bear in mind throughout any legal negotiation is that a solicitor 'must act towards other solicitors with complete frankness and good faith consistent with his overriding duty to his client' (principle 16.01, Solicitors' Practice Rules). Fraudulent or deceitful conduct by one solicitor towards another will leave the offending solicitor open to disciplinary action. Solicitors are required to keep their word, maintain personal integrity and observe good manners and courtesy towards other members of the profession, no matter how bitter the feelings between their clients. These principles should be remembered throughout any negotiation. Take advice about what is acceptable conduct if you are in any doubt about what to do, or feel uncomfortable with your client's instructions.

1.5 SUMMARY

Because negotiations form such an important part of our day to day lives, both professional and personal, it is worth while taking the time needed to understand fully the process, different strategies and the tactics which can be used. The more you invest in planning and understanding your own and others' motivations and developing your communication skills, the better you will be at negotiating.

The book is structured so that, having been introduced to the skills and qualities which you will need to be an effective negotiator (chapter 2), you can then turn to consider the strategic (chapter 3) and tactical (chapter 4) decisions you will need to make. In chapter 5 the process of negotiating is described so that you can obtain an overview of it. There then follow three chapters dealing with the more personal aspects of negotiating, chapter 6 on personal styles, chapter 7 on psychological aspects and chapter 8 on persuasion. Next follow two chapters introducing important considerations in respect of team negotiations (chapter 9) and culture and its impact on negotiations (chapter 10). No text on negotiation would be complete without an introduction to alternative dispute resolution (chapter 11). Finally, because there are strong reasons for believing that you can only understand the complexities of preparing for a negotiation once you understand the intricacies of the process, comes the chapter on preparation and checklists to help you organise your approach in a structured way (chapter 12). Lastly, a short additional reading list is provided so that you can pursue in more detail some of the issues introduced in this book.

Chapter Two

Effective Negotiators

Effectiveness as a negotiator results from a combination of personal characteristics, qualities, skills and knowledge. Many of these characteristics are naturally present in us, others can be learned through both understanding what they are and practising their use. Few people are born effective negotiators, for most it is a learned skill. A skilful negotiator is:

> one who, through understanding the risks and opportunities associated with negotiation, and of the resources he can bring to bear, is able to take active and effective measures to protect or pursue the values and interests he has at stake (Morley, quoted in *Negotiating and Bargaining — A Handbook of Communication Skills*, ed. Owen Hargie).

One of the most difficult aspects of a negotiation is being able to control, or at least be on top of every aspect of it. The more complex and wide in scope the particular negotiation is, the more difficult it will be to cope with the intellectual demands which arise. This is largely because every negotiation will require a negotiator to process a vast quantity of information, often very quickly. For the more complex problems, it is therefore necessary to find ways to make the tasks involved feasible, and so in many cases reliance will have to be put on a team of negotiators working closely together rather than on a single negotiator failing in the final analysis because of information overload (see further chapter 9).

2.1   THE QUALITIES REQUIRED TO BE A SUCCESSFUL NEGOTIATOR

Successful negotiators tend to show a fair number of the qualities which are described here. To be successful you should aim to be: patient, willing to persevere, able to think on your feet, cool under pressure or fire, inventive, creative, capable of changing and responding to a change in the pace of the negotiating meeting, capable of manipulating the proceedings so as to hide the true value to you of some or all of the issues which are on the table, self-confident, assertive, able to take and accept criticism, able to demonstrate good active listening skills, perceptive, able to exploit power, able to show self control, able to take charge, analytical, persuasive, able to see the other side's point of view, flexible, slightly unpredictable, cautious, pleasant, tactful, reasonable, rational, realistic, ambitious, determined in the sense of having high goals, firm and resolute, able to show good business judgment, able to show that you can be unreasonable when necessary, able to show scepticism when necessary, able to feel comfortable with uncertainty and unemotional.

2.2 PARTICULAR   SKILLS   REQUIRED   TO   BE   A SUCCESSFUL NEGOTIATOR

Effective negotiators are able to work out what is going on and why and what to do about it. They tend to be able to build relationships largely through the process of exchanging information. To do this a variety of techniques will be used, designed to reduce ambiguity, clarify communications and generally to slow things down so that there is enough time to take in all that is happening.

One technique which is particularly effective is that of labelling behaviour. Here a verbal description is given to what is happening, for example instead of making a suggestion to the other side or asking a question, effective negotiators will describe what they are doing: 'If I could make a suggestion?', 'If I could ask a question?'.

Effective negotiators aiming to clarify information are likely to test their understanding of what has been said in a number of ways. They will communicate their understanding to the other side by summarising and restating what the other side has said and by showing that they understand and respect the feelings of the other side. They will recognise that the other side may not always be listening to them because they may be working out what they are going to say next, and so they will find ways to help the other side understand their position. The natural temptation to respond to a proposal with a counter-proposal will often need to be resisted. Skilled negotiators will constantly repeat the same theme so that people have time to understand their message and receive the same message from every angle. They will use an iterative process, constantly redrawing the picture within which the negotiation proceeds in the light of new information obtained.

To avoid souring relations and so making communication more difficult, skilled negotiators will tend not to treat attacks on their positions as though they were attacks either on them or on their clients. They are able to switch rapidly between different negotiation strategies (that is, between collaborative, competitive and problem solving strategies, see chapter 3).

Effective negotiators will have sufficient knowledge of all the issues involved in the particular negotiation. This is likely to involve both an understanding of the commercial context and having the technical knowledge base required to be able to contribute intelligently to the discussion on each item and to understand fully what is happening.

Skilful negotiators are not afraid to disagree because they know that sometimes compromise will not provide a reasonable solution in the long term. Equally they will not be afraid to challenge the other side's position nor to ask for an explanation of what the other side is trying to achieve. They will understand that the natural human desire to avoid confrontation and conflict by agreeing may not result in a solution which is actually acceptable and so they will not slip into an agreement just to avoid the discomfort of not agreeing.

2.3 QUALITIES INDICATING POOR NEGOTIATING ABILITY

People who have been identified as generally not being very successful negotiators are those who: show eagerness to please, are rigid in their thinking, or are aggressive. Failing to prepare properly and so being unsure of the facts, the client's instructions and the law can completely undermine the position of a negotiator. Being inaccurate, slow to react or unable to think laterally or creatively will often lead to a poor result.

2.4   THE IMPACT OF STRESS

Negotiations can go wrong because it is so easy just to disagree with what the other side is saying that the whole process can degenerate into argument or conflict. Conflict situations can cause extreme stress and stress can lead people to make mistakes because the anxiety which is caused by stress can interfere with a person's ability to control his or her behaviour or to understand or respond appropriately to what the other side is saying. Effective negotiators will therefore attempt to use their communication skills to prevent arguments and so reduce the risks of conflict and consequential stress.

2.5   SUMMARY

The qualities and characteristics required to be a successful, effective and skilful negotiator are those largely associated with being a good communicator. In chapter 8 there are a number of suggestions about how to improve your comunication skills. In the next chapter you will see that your effectiveness at negotiating individual matters will be very much affected by your choice of strategy and the skills required to carry through your chosen strategy.

sitting with your back to the door is probably the least powerful position in the room to choose. Sitting your opponent in the glare of strong sunlight, thereby making it difficult for him/her to see everything that is happening is one way to improve your power and upset the other side. Remember though, that you may one day have to negotiate at your opponent's office and the trick can be played back on you! The temperature — warm or cold, the nature and timing of any refreshments and whether or not to allow people to smoke, are all part of the way you can influence or undermine the comfort and confidence of the other side (see 5.1.1).

If you meet this kind of situation, you can try to counteract it by saying that you are finding the environment uncomfortable and that you would, for example, like to break so that you can have a cigarette, or that you would like to change your seat because you are finding the sun in your eyes very disruptive.

4.2 STARTING THE BALL ROLLING

The initial moves in a legal negotiation are extremely important since they will set the parameters within which any deal will be made.

Committing to a strategy

If you intend to use a problem solving or co-operative strategy then an opening in which you clearly seek the other side's commitment to this approach will be helpful. Your aim will be to encourage the other side to declare whether or not they are willing to work *with* *you* to resolve the issues.

Who should make the first move?

The first issue to consider is who should open the process by setting out his/her client's needs, expectations and aspirations? If you consider that the other side has the stronger case, then it will often be useful for you to get the other side to begin. There are a number of ways in which you can try to do this, apart from asking them to begin. If you have set an agenda which you can get them to agree, the first item on it might be 'Opening statement from X (the other side)'. If there is no agenda or when the other side gives no sign that they are about to state their position, you can use silence and body language to indicate that they should start the process. A further alternative, rather than starting yourself, is to put to them what you think their client's case is. If your view is badly adrift from how the other side sees the situation, they are likely to come back pretty quickly to say so, and then you can legitimately ask them what they were thinking of instead (see 5.1.2 and 5.2).

4.3   BIDDING OR THE DEMAND SEQUENCE

The tactics you adopt here will be intended to establish your relative strength in the negotiating process and help you to avoid giving an impression of weakness.

Opening bids

There is a great deal of research (see D. G. Pruitt, *Negotiation Behaviour*) which indicates that the final outcome of the negotiation will be enhanced if you begin by making high demands. To start with a bid which closely approximates to where you hope to end up, will strike the other party as a weak opening move and leave you with little room for manoeuvre. The other side may then automatically increase their opening demands and revise their optimum deal to reflect the belief that they can do better than they had imagined against you. Although your opening bid should be a high one, it should not be ridiculously so. Research suggests (see references in Pruitt, *Negotiation Behaviour*, and Morley, 'Negotiating and Bargaining' in *A Handbook of Communication Skills*) that those who significantly over-estimate their opening bid do less well in terms of the final outcome of the negotiation. This is probably because they will have to move further in the concession exchange pattern, giving an overall impression of weakness (see 5.3).

Bunching

It is also often suggested that a good tactic is for you to put all your most important demands together, at an early stage in the negotiation, hence bunching. This is sometimes referred to as 'bombing' and its purpose is to 'hit' the other side with the majority of the points on which you will not be prepared to give an inch at an early stage in the proccess. It operates as though it were a high opening demand and shows strength. The risk inherent in this strategy is that you will have alerted the other side to the issues which are of major importance to your client at a point in the process when they may not have worked this out for themselves. The benefit is that, if they will not agree under any circumstances to any one of your major demands, then you can avoid wasting time by negotiating about the more minor issues.

False demands, straw issues or diversionary tactics

Another tactic is for you to make a number of false demands. These demands can bolster your client's case making your opening bid stronger than it really is. The demands you make will provide you with a broad range of issues that you will eventually (happily) concede without any problem being caused for your client, and they can also be used to put the other side off the scent of what really matters to your client. To counteract this tactic you can seek verification of their demands, by constantly asking 'why'. Do not automatically trust what the other side tells you. Check their facts.

4.4 DURING THE NEGOTIATING PROCESS

A descriptive title has been given to each of the tactics included in this section; some of these titles originated in a paper (*The Art of Negotiation*, unpublished) written by Nigel Graham Maw (Senior Partner, Rowe & Maw).

Leapfrogging

This tactic involves jumping or 'leapfrogging' from one point to another. It can be used to disguise some of the weaknesses in your case or to divert attention from them. This is a particularly useful tactic when your case is coming under sustained attack.

Let's not beat about the bush

This tactic is used to make clear to the other side that your opening statement of what your client wants is also your final position. The value of the tactic relies on an appeal to their good sense in seeing the importance of keeping control of time and therefore costs by not entering into a pointless and largely traditional concession trade. This kind of tactic only works if the other side believes you when you say that this is your first and also your final offer, and you must be willing to withdraw from the negotiation if they in turn treat it as an opening bid from you. If you come to use this tactic regularly you will gain a reputation for negotiating in this way, and consequently the other side will be encouraged to see your offer as precisely what it is, a 'close out'. You can try to counteract this tactic by ignoring the statement, either by pretending that you did not hear it, or by introducing some ideas of your own about where the bounds of the agreement should lie. You will need to look for ways to help the other side to save face if you want them to be able to move from their opening position.

The package deal

Using this tactic ensures that the other side is aware from the very beginning that you will only agree once all the component parts of the deal are in place, so that, when the package is viewed as a whole, it is considered acceptable to your client. You will want to use this tactic as a way of protecting your client's interests when you are concerned that the other side seems to have the stronger bargaining power.

Putting price last

This tactic is really an example of the way in which the package deal works. It works as an appeal to common sense aimed at helping you to resist any pressure to agree a price until you have all the other parts in place. After all, no reasonable or objective person would expect you to agree to the price until you know what the deal is!

Slice at a time or nibbling

Using this tactic means putting forward your demands one at a time, negotiating an outcome on each point before moving on to the next, until you have achieved everything you set out to achieve. By moving slowly from point to point you will be trying to disguise from the other side how much they have given. If you meet this kind of tactic, one way of combating it is to use the package deal tactic; insist on establishing all the other side's demands first and then respond to them only when you know their whole proposal. Generally you will want to use this tactic when most of the concessions are being made to you.

The tough issues

This tactic aims to help you to succeed in agreeing the issues which you see as likely to be the toughest by creating an atmosphere in which concessions are given. To set the appropriate atmosphere consider beginning the trade in concessions with one on which you can give a little, followed by an issue where you would expect to get a little, and then, once the climate is open to trading concessions, move straight on to the toughest issue, and then take the remaining issues in diminishing order of toughness.

Lack of authority or refer upstairs

This tactic can be very useful as a way of squeezing a little bit extra from the other side because, just when they think that you are moving towards finalising the deal, you say that you must go back to your client for authority to accept what they are offering. You may also use this to stall for time so as to give yourself more thinking time. To avoid this tactic being used against you, always begin by establishing what authority the other side has to conclude the deal, and unless pressed, keep back what your own authority is. One way of counteracting this tactic is to take the same opportunity to reconsider the deal and make sure that they know that this is what you are doing.

I only have X% of the price

This is a take it or leave it tactic. It assumes that everything else has been agreed and so the pressure is really on the other side to accept because otherwise they will have wasted their time and effort on issues agreed so far. This tactic is similar to the 'let's not beat about the bush' tactic, but instead of coming at the beginning of the process, it comes at the end.

The deadline

This is a very useful tactic to bring pressure to bear on the other side. Concessions tend to be made faster the closer the deadline comes. You can try to counteract this kind of tactic by finding out why there is a deadline. If there is a genuine reason, and you want the deal, you will be put under enormous pressure to agree. If you do not want the deal at any price, then you can refuse to be pressurised and hope that the other side will continue to negotiate. Creating false deadlines is a tactic beloved of the competitive negotiator. If the deadline is not genuine, you can try to change the strategy which the other side is using from competitive to problem solving by using negotiation jujitsu.

Flattery

Flattery is a very useful tactic. It can be achieved both with the words that you use and by the non-verbal clues that you give. If you flatter the other side into believing that they have made some good points, or have managed to argue you into a corner from which you cannot escape, they will feel less threatened and more willing to allow you some of your points. By showing respect for the other side, particularly if their client is with them, they will feel good about the negotiation and about themselves, and so be more likely to be helpful to you. Use this tactic preferably early in the process and very sparingly, otherwise it will begin to seem false. You can also encourage the other side to see you in a flattering light, by emphasising your past achievements.

The freeze out

By contrast, if you freeze them out by ridiculing their arguments, suggesting that they do not know what they are talking about and beating them at every point they make, you will undermine their confidence. You may even appeal to their client for a more common sense and appropriate response, and in this way you may be able to break the relationship of confidence between your opponent and his/her client, thereby enhancing your own client's cause. This is a competitive tactic. Beware of using this tactic, for if you overuse it, you may antagonise your opponent to the extent that he or she walks out; and always remember that your opponent will be unlikely to forgive you and you will almost certainly meet again! To counteract this tactic, explicitly recognise its use.

Collision course

This is useful when you are really trying to pressurise the other side, when perhaps there are several others who want, at least in theory, to 'do the deal'. Here you will deliberately lead the other side to the point where they must either give in to all your demands or walk away from the deal. This is an appropriate tactic when your client will only deal on his/her terms and is simultaneously negotiating with several different groups of people who may be willing to 'do the deal'. Alternatively, your client may not care whether or not the deal is done. This is a competitive tactic and arguably is not negotiating at all, but more in the nature of an auction.

What can I offer?

This is a useful tactic to employ when the other side is using competitive tactics and making huge demands on you; in effect, you will be asking them to say precisely what you will need to offer in order to reach some agreement.

Hit and run

This tactic is particularly useful when you have been instructed by your client to insist on a particular point. You simply say to the other side that your client insists on this point and so there is no point in discussing it. You therefore assume that it is agreed and move the negotiation on to deal with other issues.

Contrived confusion

Using this tactic is handy where the other side makes a good point which you are not willing to concede directly; instead, you pretend that they are not making any sense to you. Your response operates as a riposte to their point and even though you may have to give in, you will not appear to be doing so, thereby seeking to maintain your reputation for firmness (see chapter 6 on personal styles).

The mythical or real competitor

This tactic seeks to play off the other side against an outsider, real or imagined. Its aim is to encourage the other side to believe you when you say that you have made your final offer, or that you have reached your bottom line. They should therefore be much more aware of the risk that they will lose because there is someone else in the running.

Giveaways

The very nature of a negotiation will mean that you have to make some concessions. Plan carefully what they are to be (see chapter 12 on preparation) and introduce some false ones into your planning. Keep a running total of the points you have given to the other side and be ready to remind them of what you have given. The more you can build this up, the more you will increase the other side's sense of achievement and hence their willingness to accommodate you. You can also build up the importance of the giveaways, again in order to enhance the other side's sense of success. If they are trying to build up the value of their giveaways, minimise their value to you. It is sometimes worth fighting really hard over some of the points which you will in any event give away because of the impression this will create. The other side may think that if you are willing to fight so hard on the small points, if there is to be an agreement in the end, they will have to make the concessions.

The objective standard

This tactic enables you to cite law, commercial practice, industrial practice, morality, and indeed anything which enables you to introduce an objective standard, outside the immediate context of the negotiation, to justify your standpoint. Splitting the difference is often an example of a reasonable and objective approach to solving a problem. To counteract this tactic, try arguing that the situation you are dealing with is different, or a special case. Fisher and Ury would not describe this as a tactic, but as a necessary stage in the problem solving approach to negotiation. (See chapter 3 on negotiation strategies.) It is equally useful in competitive and collaborative negotiations.

The note

Only pass a note when you want the other side to see what is in it, otherwise they will think that you have been taken by surprise.

The caucus

Generally this tactic works best when it is you who encourage the other side to take a break because this will suggest that their case is weak and needs more time to be worked on. You might say, for example, 'you might find it helpful to take a few minutes to discuss our suggestion on . . .'. If you feel you need to discuss any of the issues raised with your own side, rather than requesting a break, find a diplimatic way of leaving the negotiation room. You will need to have rehearsed with your side precisely what you want to achieve, so that no one on your team misinterprets the message. You might say something like, 'I think it's time I at least took a natural break . . .', at which point you would hope that your side would stand up in unison to leave the room, with the aim of having an opportunity for a quick debrief and to agree tactics for the next stage.

Yes and . . .

A common way of responding to a suggestion from the other side (unless of course you are fully in agreement with them) is to say 'yes, but . . .', meaning 'I see what you mean but there are some problems with your suggestion for my client'. The other side may only hear the disagreement element which this response suggests. If instead you try saying 'yes, and . . .' you will introduce your reservations as positive conjunctive points and so there will be a better chance that the other side will be receptive to your views.

Taking minutes

Perhaps it is not wholly accurate to describe this as a tactic, but it is nevertheless very useful because it will provide proof that what you believe has been agreed genuinely has been so agreed. It will avoid the situation arising where the other party says, 'We did not actually agree that, it was merely an understanding which depends on everything else being agreed'.

Re-opening

You can use this tactic to unnerve the other side by returning to issues which were settled either to re-open them, or to deny that they were ever settled.

Finding a new way to package what you want

This tactic aims purely to help save face for the other side. This means that, whilst agreeing ostensibly to what they are saying, you produce a way which enables you to get what you want, although it appears that they have not changed their position. An example might be where they are saying that the price is not negotiable and, instead of arguing over whether the price is or is not negotiable, you find some alternative way of achieving a reduction in the price. You could, for example, propose payment by instalments over a fairly long period of time, or a discount for early payment.

Carelessness

It can sometimes be a good move for the other side not to see you as an invincible negotiator, so if you make the occasional (deliberate!) mistake you will make them feel better and so more willing to compromise.

Good guy/bad guy

This tactic is particularly well loved by police television dramas and competitive negotiators. It relies on there being at least two people in your team, one of whom takes a particularly competitive approach to the negotiation, often to the extent of alienating the other side. The second member of the team will then eventually take over the lead role, rejecting the style and approach taken by the first. The 'good guy' will build rapport with the other side on the basis of the concessions offered which will be better than those offered by the 'bad' guy, but even so fairly small. The other side will want to keep the bad guy out of it, because they will imagine that they will get less from him or her and so will rather do business with the good guy even if the good guy offers very little.

The walkout

If you intend to use this tactic, you must have your client's full support and your client must be prepared for the possibility that the other side will not cave in and agree on your terms. If you want to leave the door open a fraction, then you must be careful to make quite specific what the conditions are so that you can come back to the negotiation table without losing face. This is a competitive tactic. However, be careful when using it; see the decision in *Goff* v *Gauthier* (1991) 62 P & CR 388.

Aggression

This tactic requires you to act aggressively, threatening the other side and trying to force them into capitulating. Aggression, to be effective, must be realistic and any threats must be capable of being carried out if necessary.

Humour

As a tactic, humour can help break deadlock and tension. More generally, it helps maintain rapport, and a cordial atmosphere, a sense of community of ideas, 'togetherness' and warmth. It is particularly helpful if you have chosen to use either the collaborative or problem solving strategic approach.

The summary

This can be very useful in a long negotiation or where the discussion appears to be somewhat rudderless, when it is helpful to summarise the common ground between the parties, expressed from your point of view. This does not mean that you will seek to misrepresent what has been agreed, but whoever has charge of the summary can slant things in their direction.

4.5 MODES OF NEGOTIATING AS TACTICS

4.5.1 Face to face communication

Face to face contact in a meeting around or across a table is much better if you want to keep control of the process and avoid delays. It is much easier to build a relationship with the other side and a good atmosphere in which the negotiation can proceed when you meet them face to face. Usually meetings will be planned and so you will have time to ensure that you are adequately prepared before meeting. You will be able to take in both visually and aurally all possible sources of information indicating how the other side feels and what really matters to them, as you will be able to take account of both verbal and non-verbal communication. It is also much harder to say 'no' in a face to face meeting. If the meeting is at your office, however, it is rather difficult to use the walkout tactic.

4.5.2   Written communication

Negotiating through written communications creates difficulties in building rapport and can be quite slow, as you will have to wait for a response to your last communication, despite the fax! The advantages of negotiating in this way include your ability to choose your words very carefully and ensure that you say precisely what you intend to say and that you have a written record of precisely what you did say. You will always be able to ensure that you are properly prepared before replying. If you want to cease negotiations because your client is not happy with the proposals being put by the other side, you have the choice either of communicating your client's withdrawal from the negotiation or of just not replying to their last communication (but note principle 16.02 of the Guide to Professional Conduct). There will always be a clear written record of precisely what has or has not been agreed.

There are also a number of disadvantages. You may have to disclose your own position before having any clear idea of where the other side stands. Once you have put into writing what your client will be prepared to do, it will be difficult to change position. If you fail to use grammar, punctuation and words well, it could put your client in some difficulty if what you have written turns out not to reflect what you meant to say. You will have less opportunity to understand what the other side is really thinking unless they are totally honest and straightforward in their communications with you.

4.5.3 The telephone

Negotiating by telephone again leaves you unable (in the present state of technology) to see the non-verbal responses of the other side to the points that you raise. It is then not so easy to build rapport unless you have met in the past and are merely continuing the negotiation by telephone. There are certain advantages, however, to using the telephone since you can ensure that you are properly prepared before you pick up the telephone and may be able to take the other side by surprise. You can also bring the discussion to an end very easily, the equivalent of the walkout would be purely to put the telephone down. You can also tell them that you will get back to them when you have had time to take instructions or have thought about what they have said.

The major disadvantage is that you will have no confirmation of what was agreed or even discussed. This can be a real problem since it is very difficult to hold the other side to anything if they later deny having agreed the point, unless you have conducted the discussion with the loud speaker on and a third party taking a note, or have recorded the conversation (which incidentally should only be done if you have first told the other side's solicitor that this is what you intend to do). You should consider having your client with you so that you can get an immediate response to the suggestions being made by the other side, particularly if the other side has their client with them.

4.6 SUMMARY

In this chapter you have been encouraged to think about the many ways in which you can influence the course which a negotiation follows, either by using or recognising the tactics which could affect you or the other side. It has also been suggested that, if you are aware of the tactics which the other side is using to try to affect you, that will take you much of the way down the road of combating the tactic.

You have also been given some ideas about which tactics are likely to be most appropriate at different phases of the negotiating process and which can be related to a particular negotiating strategy. Some of the tactics described are particularly useful when you are using a competitive strategy, others are designed largely to combat a competitive strategy. It should also be remembered that Fisher and Ury suggest that if you choose to use a problem-solving strategy should not use any tricks — using the idea of what y precisely what you get. Whether you follow their adv.   not, understanding tactics and knowing what their possible im   will be on the negotiating process can only help your proficiency.

Now that the best strategy to use has been considered, and the tactics required to put it into effect have been discussed, the following chapter provides an analysis of the process of negotiation.

settlement are recorded appropriately. This may be through an exchange of letters, a deed of agreement, draft minutes of order to put before the judge for approval, a draft *Tomlin* order or a final version of a commercial agreement. Whatever the appropriate format is, it is crucial to ensure that the record is clear and gives effect to what has been agreed.

5.7 SUMMARY

In this chapter the way in which most negotiations will unfold has been described. You will need to ensure that you are well prepared for each phase of the process so that you are ready to participate fully and effectively in every aspect of it. (See chapter 12 on preparation.) If you are going to make concessions, make sure you know what they are to be and when and why you are going to make them. There is some important evidence (see chapter 7 on psychological aspects) suggesting that the way you concede will influence the other side's perception of you and of your personal style, and will enable them to identify possible pyschological advantage.

Chapter Six

Personal Styles

In this chapter the main personal operating styles which you are likely to meet in the negotiations you see and/or take part in are described. The aim in describing these types is to encourage you to be aware of the impact which different personal operating styles can have on the potential outcome of a case, so that you can think about how you should appear when planning your own approach. Although there are two obvious and opposite types of character set, namely being either hard and tough or soft, there is one further style which seems to be particularly important for the potential success of a negotiation, and this is a firm and resolute approach.

6.1 HARD AND TOUGH

Hard and tough negotiators you will find are generally not easily intimidated. They will not stray far from their original demands and tend to offer only very few, and usually only very small concessions. They tend to reduce the size or value of the concessions they give the longer the negotiation continues, therefore the overwhelming message they give to the other side is that it is the other side who must give the most concessions if there is finally to be any kind of agreement. Hard negotiators are not easily threatened and are unlikey to respond, in the sense of giving in, to threats of deadlock or ending the negotiation process. Tough negotiators have very high expectations of the outcome of the negotiation. Competitive negotiators tend to be, or to be seen as tough.

articulate the differences between their respective positions, the more likely they are to reach an agreement which is acceptable to them both. Problem solving negotiators tend to adopt a firm and resolute style.

6.7 YOUR PERSONAL STYLE

What personal style are you most comfortable with? Whatever your answer, you can always work on your personal style and try to change your natural personal preference. This is possible where you make a determined and practised attempt to change your character, or because change becomes possible as a direct result of the particular atmosphere operating in a negotiation, or as a direct result of the style adopted by the other side. Research evidence (described by D. G. Pruitt, (*Negotiation Behaviour*) suggests that many negotiators will react to a tough style and the absence of generosity by becoming softer and demonstrating their own generosity. Consequently, some negotiators will reward a tough style with the opposite style, softness. The reverse is also often true. When a negotiator is met with an unexpectedly soft opening, he or she is more likely to meet that opening with a much tougher response than was originally planned, and so will become much tougher. Be aware of these tendencies, and plan your responses to them accordingly.

6.8 SUMMARY

In this chapter it has been suggested that there are three basic personal behaviour preferences which you are likely to meet or adopt during a negotiation. The aim is for you to understand the possible risks and advantages which these styles can have for you. Your personal behavioural preference should be kept closely controlled if, in allowing it to dominate your behaviour, you are likely to be put at a disadvantage. Clearly the most important message you can give to the other side is that you are firm and resolute. This will prevent them from seeing you as likely to be weak and therefore easily dominated in the negotiation process.

Chapter Seven

Psychological Aspects

There is much to learn from the work of pyschologists on interpersonal interaction. Research into negotiating behaviour is just one area of the work in this field. There are a number of interesting studies which explain some of the psychological aspects which can influence the outcome of the negotiating process. You should always keep these ideas in mind when preparing for, planning and carrying through a negotiation. Many of the ideas mentioned in this chapter originate in the interesting books and articles published by Dean G. Pruitt and by Ian Morley and in the work of Fisher and Ury. You will find the full references to these in the bibliography at the end of the book. References to research evidence are those described by Pruitt (*Negotiation Behaviour*), by Morley and Hosking (*A Social Psychology of Organising*) and by Morley ('Negotiating and Bargaining' in *A Handbook of Communication Skills*).

7.1 WHAT DRIVES US?

The driving force in most of us is that we would rather win than lose. It is therefore valuable to recognise this human element both in ourselves and in others because it aids our understanding of the interpersonal interactions which can influence the outcome of a negotiation. Both you and your opponent will want to succeed, be it for yourselves, for your clients and/or for your firms or chambers. If you want to encourage the other side to reach any kind of agreement or settlement with you, it will help if you can ensure at least some successes for them and their client. If they feel that they will gain little or nothing from the negotiation, they will be far less likely to agree or recommend the deal to their client. A face saving formula which allows the other side to return with at least some triumphs will be more likely to lead to an agreement. (For further discussion see Fisher and Brown, *Getting Together: Building a Relationship that Gets to Yes*.)

7.2 THE ROLE WHICH EMOTION PLAYS

It is also important to recognise and understand the role which both your and their emotion can play in a negotiation. It is well understood that people will sometimes act emotionally and irrationally when in pursuit of some particular purpose. Negotiations can create the environment for just such a response and you will find that some of your opponents will become emotional and irrational primarily because they are unable to separate their own personal desire to win from the substance of the issues which are being negotiated. Emotions can have a distorting effect and can create negative feelings of, for example, insecurity, hopelessness, helplessness, rejection or hostility. Emotions can also sometimes have a positive effect by creating a sense of security, optimism, confidence, respect or concern. The issue for you then is how to deal with emotions be they your own or those of the other side.

Before you can deal with emotions you will first need to be able to recognise them. You must get to know yourself so that you are able to recognise when you, yourself, are responding irrationally or emotionally to the other side and/or their proposals. Watch yourself and identify the non-verbal clues to your own emotional temperature. At the same time be aware of their emotions by relating what you know about the clues to your own emotional behaviour to them. Listen carefully to them so that you hear both the overt and the more covert meaning of what they are saying. Test whether your interpretation of their emotional state is right; simply ask them whether your analysis of their emotional state is correct. Learn how to control your emotions and how to help others to do so. Emotional situations can sometimes be brought under control by taking a break, by counting to ten, or by using or allowing yourself to be used as a sounding board. Realise that emotions such as fear, anger or frustration can disrupt an otherwise calm and competent performance.

One very successful way of dealing with emotions which are interfering with the negotiating process is to make emotions explicit. You can do this by acknowledging emotion as legitimate by, for example, referring to your side's emotional feelings explicitly and by trying to avoid blaming the other side for them. You should aim not simply to express your feelings but also to acknowledge their existence and to explain them to the other side. You will need to accept responsibility for them and where necessary apologise for them or for contributing to the other side's emotional response.

It is generally better for human relations if reason and emotion are in balance. This is more likely to be the case when such feelings are explicitly accepted as worthy and are seen to be valued. In the long term, emotional coercion will be likely to cause more problems than it will solve. It is just as well to prepare for emotions before they arise and to anticipate both your own and the other side's emotional reactions. Recognise that your ability to analyse the situation will not solve a dispute if it is charged with emotion.

7.3   GOOD RELATIONS WITH THE OTHER SIDE

There is much evidence to suggest that the better your relationship is with the other side, the better you will serve your client's interests. Therefore, the more you can do to improve the interaction between the parties, the more likely you are to be successful in the negotiation process. Developing a good relationship with the other side will depend largely on the early stages of the negotiation and on the atmosphere created at the beginning of the process. There is evidence to suggest that we are likely to be particularly helpful to people we like, to those with whom we can empathise and to those on whom we are dependent for future benefits and when we are in a good mood!

You should therefore consider carefully how you can best build a good relationship with the other side. Much will depend on how well you communicate with the other side; the better your communication skills are, the easier it will be to build a relationship with the other side. Consider ways to engender a sense in the other side that you view them with respect. You can do this by ensuring that you listen well to them and hear all that they are saying about their and their client's needs and that they know that you have heard them.

There is also some evidence to suggest that negotiators will make faster concessions to people with whom they feel they have a common bond. So, if you can engender that sense of a common bond, you should be able to improve the deal you reach with the other side and the time which it takes to get there.

7.4 PERCEPTIONS

Each of us, as we observe any event, will focus our attention on different aspects of that event and will then tend to reach conclusions based mainly on the evidence which we have identified as supporting our particular point of view. All of us will sometimes exhibit this kind of selective memory! Part of the reason why we select only limited elements of an event is because it helps us to remember information. We filter and label information and try to fit it into a coherent story. The more information we obtain, the more work we have to do to synthesise it with what we already know. We will tend to do this by reshaping the information we already have to fit in with the new information.

It has already been suggested that one of the most difficult aspects of negotiating is the extent to which you will have to assimilate information rapidly as you obtain it from the other side. Your perceptions can influence the extent to which you obtain an accurate picture of the situation and are able to respond to it. One way of avoiding allowing your perceptions to cloud the truth is to use reflective listening (see chapter 8 on persuasion), where you will constantly be checking the accuracy of what you believe you have heard with the other side until you have got it quite right.

7.5   TRUST

We will tend to trust everyone simply because we would like
everyone to trust us, at least until they prove us wrong! You must,
however, recognise the risks which you are likely to run if you are
automatically too trusting.

7.6   MIRRORING OR MATCHING AND MIS-MATCHING BEHAVIOUR

Mirroring or matching behaviour occurs when we copy the
behaviour pattern which is being used by the other side. This is
particularly likely if we believe the other side to be behaving badly.
We will ask ourselves why we should behave better than the other
side. What can happen then is that a behaviour pattern will be set up
which can become increasingly hostile. This creates potential risks
for the effectiveness of a negotiation, because where a pattern of
hostility is set up, anger will become the dominating emotion. When
angry, we tend to listen only to ourselves and not to the other side
and consequently will tend to misunderstand what the other side is
saying and believe that they are being deceitful and that we are
being coerced. We will tend to see their conduct as worse than our
own and gradually we will find ourselves in a downward spiral in
which a pattern of retaliation becomes the norm.

We will feel justified in adopting this behaviour pattern because in
effect we will merely be reciprocating. Reciprocity is seen as a
generally accepted standard of fairness and so it provides a very
useful excuse to explain our behaviour. We are therefore likely to
believe that it is alright to respond to a competitive strategy by being
just as competitive in return. Research suggests that even if you
believe that your behaviour is as good as the other side's, they are
likely to see it as worse.

Apart from its potential impact on the atmosphere of the
negotiation and negotiation strategy used, matching behaviour can
also explain the way in which concessions are given (see chapter 6 on
personal styles). There is evidence to suggest that the more the
other side demands, the more you are likely to demand and that the
faster the other side concedes, the faster you are likely to concede.

This is a fairly common behaviour pattern and is sometimes referred to as strategy imitation, but it is by no means a universal one.

The alternative behaviour pattern is mis-matching. This occurs when one party demands more when the other side's demands are smaller, and concedes faster when the other side fails to concede. Mis-matching is commonly seen whenever time pressure is high. Initial demands are more likely to mis-match. When negotiating, be aware of your own tendency to match or mis-match the other side's concession pattern and their tendency to match or mis-match with you.

7.7   SELF-ESTEEM AND IMAGE LOSS

There is a weight of evidence to suggest that people with low self-esteem or who fear loss of self-esteem are much more reluctant to change their minds in a dispute because they fear losing face. This can have an impact on the way in which a negotiation unfolds. Starting with a high demand and conceding only slowly is often tied up with a negotiator's desire not to lose face in the negotiating process.

Negotiators may be particularly concerned about the possibility of image loss if they are negotiating in a team or accompanied by their client. They will also be concerned to promote a firm image because they will be keen to avoid a reputation for weakness which could be used by others against them in future negotiations. Negotiators will try to avoid looking weak in front of their clients or colleagues. To protect image in these circumstances, a negotiator may turn to methods to try to rectify image loss, such as threatening or making counter-threats or refusing to make any more concessions.

7.8   CONCESSIONS AND SACRIFICE

Concessions and sacrifices can have a very significant impact on the image of a negotiator. Image loss occurs when concessions are given. Where large concessions are given or more concessions are given than are given by the other side, the image loss will be greater. This of itself can be enough to inhibit concession making. Negotiators who make an early sacrifice in their position tend to jeopardise their reputation for resolve because their opponents will assume that there is more to come provided that they keep up the pressure. On the other hand, negotiators who stand firm for too long may risk being seen as totally intransigent and as an impossible opponent. Consequently, a negotiator who wants to reach agreement in a hurry will want to avoid the dual hazards of either conceding too slowly or conceding too fast.

Negotiators who make larger initial demands, or smaller concessions will achieve the larger eventual outcome. Negotiators who make moderate demands will usually achieve the best outcomes when compared with those who demand little (who generally reach agreement, but with only a limited value in terms of outcome) and those who demand too much, who will often fail to reach agreement at all.

Negotiators tend to concede less and make more threats when their opponent seems to be withholding concessions with the aim of gaining an unfair advantage.

There is evidence to suggest that reflecting behaviour will tend to foster concession making. Reflecting behaviour occurs when you listen carefully to the views of the other side and then repeat back to them what you believe their view to be until the other side is happy that you have accurately reflected their point of view.

7.9   EXPECTATIONS ABOUT THE OTHER SIDE'S DEMANDS

Negotiators will tend to decide how much to demand and what to concede on the basis of what they assume they can expect the other side to demand or concede. The more they expect the other side to concede, the more they will demand from the other side and the less they will concede. Be aware of this tendency as you prepare for negotiating and recognise that you may have to explain why the other side's expectations in respect of your concession pattern are misplaced, otherwise there is a risk that they will be completely wrong-footed and that this could undermine the negotiation.

7.10 SETTING LIMITS

Most negotiators will set a number of limits before beginning to negotiate. They will set an opening level, which will usually be quite some distance from where they expect to end up; there will be an ideal level at which it is hoped to be able to settle; and there will be a bottom line which is the level below which settlement becomes impossible. The further your opening bid is from your ideal result, the greater will be your room for manoeuvre. Consider whether there will be any advantage to you in making an unrealistically high opening bid. You may want to use it as a means of obscuring your actual limits from the other side. If they make an opening bid which you think is very high, consider whether they are trying a feint to obscure the reality from you. Negotiators who set limits will tend to make more rapid concessions than those who set no limits at all.

7.11 TIME PRESSURE

Time limits can be used to create immense pressure in a negotiation. Time pressure will generally result in lower demands being made and faster concessions. This is particularly so where there is a substantial difference between the opening bid and the ideal level where time pressure seems to increase the rate of concession making. Time can be used very effectively as a tactic to force concessions from the other side. Where time pressure is greater on the other side than on you, you can attempt to increase the pressure on them by slowing the process down. Where time pressure is greater on you than it is on the other side, then try to ensure that you keep the pace up, otherwise you may end up feeling under even greater pressure and so be more likely to concede more than you wanted.

7.12 REPRESENTING ANOTHER'S INTERESTS

Lawyers who negotiate in their capacity as lawyers will nearly always do so as the representative of someone else; in effect they champion other people's interests rather like the knights of old. This can have an influence on the way in which lawyers negotiate. Negotiators assume that their clients will take a more competitive stance than they would normally do themselves. This assumption has an impact on the negotiating process in that, to please their clients, negotiators will make higher demands and concede more slowly. The process can therefore often take much longer than was expected.

When clients are present at the negotiation, this in itself may cause negotiators to become more competitive because they will want to emphasise their strength both to the other side and to their client. Where negotiators believe that their client has a lower status than they have, they are likely to be less overawed by their client, and so not as competitive as they would be if they see their client as having a higher or equal status to them.

The more motivated you are to please your client, perhaps because you want to retain them as clients, the more likely it is that you will be competitive towards the other side. They will have similar motivations to you and could be equally determined to present an image to their client throughout the negotiation which they believe their client will find appealing.

7.13 SUMMARY

The aim of this chapter has been to encourage you to recognise that the research into negotiations by psychologists can be very useful to you both in preparing for a negotiation and in understanding what is happening during the negotiation process. If you think about these issues, you will be better prepared and also better able to analyse and respond to problems as they arise.

Chapter Eight

Persuasion

8.1 PERSUASION OR COERCION?

Much of the potential success of a negotiation will depend on your ability either to persuade or to coerce the other side to your client's point of view. The approach you adopt will depend on which strategy you have decided is most appropriate to the particular negotiation.

When you have chosen to use a competitive strategy you will want to push the other side into adopting your point of view and so you will be trying to coerce them into doing so. You may seek to do this by warning them of the dire consequences of their failure to concede to you, by threatening them that if they do not do what you want you will abandon the negotiation and by extorting what you want from them.

In contrast, where you are using either a co-operative or a problem solving approach you will aim to persuade the other side to your client's point of view. The art of persuasion is made up of a number of interconnected techniques and skills aimed at ensuring good communication. Your ability to build rapport with the other side, to question effectively, to listen well, to be assertive and to use and understand non-verbal communication are all important aspects of being persuasive.

The first point to make is that you should not expect to be able to persuade everyone to your point of view, much will depend on the position from which the other side starts. If they are already largely in agreement with your point of view your task will be a fairly easy one. If they are completely at odds with your view you will be unlikely to be able to persuade them totally to change their mind; the best you can hope for is that you will be able to move them away from holding a view which is completely contrary to your own. This chapter suggests ways in which you can enhance your ability to persuade.

8.2   BUILDING RAPPORT

In chapter 5 it was suggested that you plan at the start of every negotiation to create an appropriate atmosphere. Often you will be aiming for one which is warm, friendly and businesslike. When you already know the people with whom you are to negotiate, it makes it much easier to build this kind of easy atmosphere because you will know how to ease the early part of the meeting by chatting of this and that before you get down to business. When you do not know the lawyer/s on the other side, then you should still look for ways to ease the opening stages of the negotiation. Try to arrive in plenty of time. Prior to the formal opening of the negotiation process, try and learn something of what makes the other side tick. If you can share a joke or some personal details, then this will immediately help to break the ice and you will find both sides will work together more easily. You will find that if you try to keep the other side at a distance and the atmosphere on the chilly side you will take longer to make progress. Other suggestions about how to build rapport can be found in chapter 5.

8.3   QUESTIONING

Much of what you will hope to achieve through negotiating will depend on your ability to find out as much as possible about what the other side wants. Although you will already have a pretty shrewd idea of what they want because you will have thought through the situation as much from the other side's point of view as from your own client's, even so you will want to check out your assumptions and perceptions by questioning the other side. You will want to establish why they are asking for a particular concession from you, or why they are not prepared to make a particular concession that your client wants. If you need to know about their underlying motives, do not be afraid to ask them precisely why they want something, or why they are not prepared to move on a particular issue.

There are basically three different types of question which you will find useful in negotiating. These are: the closed question, the open-ended question and the reflective question.

The closed question generally requires no more than a very straightforward answer, often either yes or no and is very useful for checking on precisely where the other side stands on a particular issue. An example might be, 'so, on the basis that our client does X and Y, your client will be happy to pay £Z?', to which the answer will be either yes or no or a variant.

There is a whole literature on the uses to which you can put yea-saying and nay-saying closed questions and they can be particularly effective in negotiations. The aim of using these kinds of questions is really to close down the discussion and force agreement with or understanding of your point of view out of the other side. They provide a very useful way of wrongfooting the other side. A couple of examples may help. If you were to say to the other side something like: 'You surely do not expect my client to be able to find the kind of money we have been discussing in two weeks?', this is a nay-saying question which aims to force the other side to agree with your proposition that your client cannot find the money required in a short time frame. An example of a yea-saying question would be: 'You would agree that my client has moved a considerable way towards meeting your demands', again in using this formulation you are endeavouring to force the other side to agree with you so that you can build on that agreement to move the negotiation on to the next issue.

Open-ended questions are much better tools for gathering information. This kind of question invites the other side to talk widely about the issues. An example would be: 'Perhaps you can explain why your client feels particularly strongly that he should keep the Spode china rather than the Wedgwood crystal?'. The aim of asking this question would be to try to understand fully the reasons underlying the other side's demands and to give further opportunities for pressing the negotiation along the desired path.

The reflective question is usually aimed at establishing whether you have accurately understood everything that the other side has been saying (i.e., both the facts and emotions underlying the situation). An example might be: 'Please correct me if I am wrong, but I get the impression from what you have said that your client is still very angry with my client for leaving him and going to live with the co-respondent, and that he consequently feels that in justice he should therefore have the lion's share of the family's assets. Am I right?'

Questions can also be used as a way of controlling the process, perhaps by encouraging the discussion to move on. Examples include questions like: 'shall we move on to consider . . ., would you like to consider issue A at the same time as we consider issue B . . ., how do you feel about our proposals on delivery, should we turn to discuss those now . . .?'

There is however a risk in relying too heavily on questioning the other side. If this approach is used too much, perhaps to the exclusion of giving any information, the other side will soon become defensive and less willing to respond. Resist the temptation to slip into the cross-examining mode unless you are trying to coerce an agreement from the other side.

The 'what if . . .?' question can be a particularly useful tool especially when you are trying to attach issues one to another. So as an example of this type of approach you could ask: 'how would you feel if we were to say that we would be willing to meet you half way on the price, if at the same time you were willing to allow us to . . .?'. You can also use the 'what if . . .?' type question when you are trying to obtain information from the other side so as to see whether the parameters of the deal can be pushed in a particular direction. An example would be: 'if we said we were willing to . . . how would you feel about that?'. Its value is that without making any concessions and therefore risking losing face, you will have moved matters on by giving the other side an understanding of what you might be willing to do, and so you have an opportunity to test the water without being committed to the move.

8.4 LISTENING

Probably one of the things most of us do least well is to listen properly to what we are being told. Hence in most books or courses on communication skills, considerable time and effort is spent trying to improve the way in which we listen. Being able to listen well is in itself a good way to develop rapport between the parties. If you make it clear that you are interested in what the other side is saying and that you have heard what they say accurately, in terms both of the verbal message and non-verbal clues they give when they are speaking and also when they are listening, you will learn more of what really matters to the other side, what their real concerns are and make them feel that they are using their time well in telling you their concerns. Knowing well what the other side want and why will place you in a better position to respond to their needs.

What can you do to improve the way you listen? Always try to listen actively. This means giving both verbal and non-verbal clues to indicate that you are listening. Try nodding from time to time as the other side speaks about their needs, or saying 'I see' or 'aha'. Keep your mind on what they are saying, do not let your mind wander, pay attention, try not to think about what you are going to say next whilst the other side is speaking, if you do, you will not hear everything that is being said. Let the other side know that you have been listening to what they say by summarising, repeating concisely what you have been told and relating what you have heard to the way your client sees things. Always observe the other side as keenly as you can. If you are taking notes try to ensure that you make your note when you have checked that what you heard was correct, rather than taking down what the other side says whilst they are speaking. If you watch them carefully, all kinds of clues relating to what they really think may become apparent to you. Try not to interrupt them when they are speaking, you may miss the vital clue to their real position. Do not jump to conclusions, test out what you think you have heard and always try to understand and check your understanding of why they are approaching the problems which they see in the particular way that they are. The other side's interests and vantage point will be different from yours and what matters at this point is that you understand their position and how it differs from yours.

8.5   PERSUADING THROUGH DISCUSSION

Here you will be aiming to persuade the other side to your client's position by educating them as to the reasons why your client is taking that particular view of the situation and the issues. Ensure that your arguments are logical and morally persuasive. You can encourage them to follow this approach by setting an example.

Once you have understood what their needs are, you can think about how you can satisfy them without suffering some disadvantage. One technique often found to be effective in persuading is to emphasise the similarities between your position and their position. If you cannot give them something that they want, rather than giving the bad news upfront, always explain what the problem is before you say you cannot do it. In your own presentation of your client's position, stick to your strongest points and arguments and repeat them as often as you can. This is often referred to as the 'broken record technique' and is used to enhance assertiveness.

If the other side asks you questions, answer them only if you are sure you understand what they want to know, and have checked that you understand their question. Think about whether it suits you to answer their questions at the time when they are asked and whether you wish to give a full answer or whether you would prefer not to take that issue at the particular time the question is asked. If you have planned to give the information once a certain stage in the negotiation process has been reached and you feel that your plans should not be changed, then stick with them.

There are a number of techniques you can use to avoid answering a question, ranging from deflecting to silence! If they make a proposal to you which your client does not like, instead of rejecting it out of hand, there are a number of ways to respond to it, for example, by making a counter proposal, or you could delay your response by keeping the question on the table but not responding to it immediately, or you could add your own conditions to it. If you make a proposal which is rejected, ask them what can be done to improve your proposal.

The importance of the discussion phase in the negotiation process has already been described, particularly if a collaborative or problem solving strategy is being used (see chapter 5). Whether or not the discussion phase will be effective will depend greatly on the extent to which you have been able to persuade the other side to accept your client's point of view on the facts, the law and/or the options. A significant element of your likely success is the way in which you are able to advocate your client's interests. So, much like the advocate in court whose main aim is to seek to persuade the trier of fact and the judge to their client's view, you will be attempting a similar task.

Much will depend on how you structure what you say and also on the way that you say it. The sections in this chapter which deal with questioning, listening, non-verbal communication and assertiveness are relevant to how you should make your points. Much can be learned from the skills you would use to make a formal presentation (see Anthony King's book in this series entitled *Effective Communication*). Alan Pannett suggests (see *Managing the Law Firm*) that you can enhance your persuasiveness by ensuring that your message is put across in a logical way which might include the following elements:

(a)   an opening statement which highlights what the potential benefit is so that your audience knows why they should listen to you;

(b)   a description of the way you see and can support the particular legal point, can establish your facts or the value of the particular option you are proposing which if accepted by the other side will be beneficial to them;

(c)   a clear statement relating the benefits of that legal point, fact or option specifically to the other side;

(d)   an explanation of the evidence which underpins those benefits as being likely to accrue to the other side if they accept and adopt the particular legal point, interpretation of fact or option you are proposing;

(e)   a statement dealing with any objections which could be raised before they raise them; and

(f)   a concise summary of the points you have made.

8.6   ASSERTIVENESS

Assertiveness can be described as the right of the individual to express his or her desires while simultaneously respecting the rights of the other people involved. It is not to be confused with aggression. To be an effective negotiator and persuader you will need to be or become assertive.

Being assertive means saying what you want clearly and firmly so that the other side fully understands what you or your client wants and why you or your client wants it. You can be as direct as you like, provided that you state clearly and succinctly your or your client's feelings, desires and perceptions. Being assertive enables you to express your own concerns without at the same time either attacking or demeaning the other person. Assertive individuals approach conflict situations with an adaptive appraisal of the situation and a realistic self-confidence in their ability to emit appropriate behaviours. To be assertive will mean showing that you are confident in as many ways as possible.

The whole purpose of using assertive behaviour is to encourage the other side to the view, both that you are entitled to hold a different view from them, and that you recogise that they have the right to hold a different view from you. It will help the other side to understand your standpoint and will encourage the other side to tell you theirs. Assertive people are direct and honest whilst showing respect for others. Being assertive can help you to resist pressure which the other side is trying to bring to bear, if it is unreasonable, because you have the right to resist unreasonable behaviour and demands. Being assertive will therefore help you to combat a competitive strategy.

Non-assertive people tend to avoid confronting the issues and will only tell you what they really think in a very indirect way, if at all. Being non-assertive will be likely to result in a win/lose situation because acting non-assertively enables the other side to win. People who are aggressive will tend to be disrespectful and will try to undermine the points being made by denying in effect that the other party is entitled to hold a view which is different from or contrary to their own. Aggressiveness communicates an impression of superiority and disrespect. It aims to enable the aggressor to get his/her own way because it allows others no choice. Its aim is to violate the rights of others. Aggressiveness as a behaviour style can be particularly useful when you are seeking a win/win outcome in a negotiation.

How can you be assertive? Assertiveness is an expressive skill, to be able to show it involves both verbal and non-verbal behaviours. A part of it will depend on how you feel, so thinking assertively and feeling confident about your ability to do so is very important. How can you change your behaviour to become more assertive? When choosing your words and describing your feelings, use words that are direct, honest, appropriate and respectful. Use 'I' statements. For example: 'I feel this discussion is getting nowhere', rather than 'you' statements as for example, in contrast: 'you are not allowing this discussion to get anywhere' (aggressive) or 'we do not seem to be getting anywhere' (non-assertive). Use factual description rather than judgments or exaggerations. Take ownership of your thoughts and feelings and express them accordingly. Use clear and direct requests when you want someone to do something for you, rather than hinting at what you want done, for example: 'please tell me whether you can raise the kind of money we are talking about', rather than 'I wonder if money could be a problem'. Say 'no' politely and firmly, be realistic, accurate and respectful, express preferences and priorities.

8.7 NON-VERBAL COMMUNICATION

Research confirms that your body language conveys a great deal of information about you and what you are thinking and feeling and hence forms an important part of the message you communicate to the other side. Your body language can help to communicate your assertiveness. Think about and practise the most appropriate body language. In general terms you should seek to show a relaxed openness by sitting back in your chair, not folding your arms in front of you and not fiddling; your hands should be open and you should face (square up to) the person on the other side to whom you are addressing your remarks. A steady tone of voice (loud enough to be easily heard), the inflections you use, the pace you use and your fluency are all important in projecting assertiveness and an image of self-confidence. How you use eye contact, which should be steady, looking people straight in the face, your facial expression, if possible calm, sincere and serious, the flexible use of gestures, movements which are inconspicuous when listening and fluid and purposeful when speaking, and your posture are all important. Your clothing and hair style are all part of how you project your personality. So if you plan and practise these elements, they will help you both to feel and communicate your assertiveness. Chapter 6, entitled *Attending Behaviour*, in Helena Twist's book, *Effective Interviewing*, provides an excellent explanation of these aspects of communicating.

8.8   BREAKING DEADLOCK

Despite every effort to reach agreement, you may on occasion find yourself making no progress, because the negotiation has deadlocked. Deadlock is likely to occur in those cases where you or the other side feel that the negotiation is failing to meet what are considered to be the minimum requirements. This may be because they have not listened properly to what you have identified as your client's minimum requirements, or because you have failed to hear what they are saying about their client's minimum requirements. In order to move things on you will therefore have to consider whether you have been using the correct strategy (see chapter 3 on negotiation strategies) and whether the atmosphere surrounding the negotiation needs to be altered so that it is more positive. It may be necessary to go at least part of the way back to the drawing board to see whether there are any other options which could solve the difficulty, it may even be possible to try brainstorming other options with the other side to see whether any progress can be made.

To identify the cause of the deadlock and discover other possible solutions, consider caucusing with your team and/or client. Taking a break from the negotiation meeting or just giving yourself and the other side some space can improve the atmosphere and give a fresh boost to the process.

To resurrect a more positive atmosphere in the negotiation, try going back over the ground which has been agreed, emphasising the purpose which has brought both sides to the negotiation table. Ask them for their help in trying to find a way forward. Try to find a way of defining the issues which have led to the deadlock in a different way. Try to move the discussion on to new areas which appear to you to be likely to be more promising of compromise or which both sides can see value in finding ways to solve because they have common interests in finding a solution to that part of the problem. Encourage the other side to recognise what the cost of failure is likely to be, especially where considerable time and effort has already been committed to the negotiation process. Use your questioning skills to try to identify as precisely as possible what the sticking point is and your listening skills to be clear that you have fully understood the point(s).

Find new ways to put across possible solutions to the problem. Suggest that a possible solution could be tried on a trial basis (if this is possible and your client agrees).

Suggest that a new negotiation team takes over and/or that negotiations are halted temporarily and that they be resumed somewhere else, on a different day and at a different time. In some cases you may be able to suggest that an expert third party be involved to propose an appropriate solution or that the matter be referred to mediation or other form of alternative dispute resolution technique (see chapter 11 on alternative dispute resolution).

8.9 HOW TO MAKE OR ENCOURAGE THE OTHER SIDE TO MAKE CONCESSIONS

There have been described in some detail in chapter 5 on process and in chapter 7 on psychological aspects, some of the issues which surround the making of concessions which is an integral part of the negotiation process. You will recall that when a negotiator makes a concession he or she will suffer, to at least some degree, a loss of face and loss of self-esteem. It is therefore important to find a way to make concessions yourself so that you suffer as little loss of face as possible and, if it is the other side that is making concessions, your role is to find a way to try to help them to do so without losing face.

You may find it helpful to find a way to rationalise your own concession making or to provide a rationale for the other side to make a concession. You might, for example, say that you had thought that the other side would expect more of 'X' than they in fact want and so, in those circumstances, it is only right that you should allow them more of 'Y' than you originally intimated was possible. You could make it easier for them by referring to recent negotiations in which you have been involved in which it has become common to do something in a particular way, the now normal way, as a way of encouraging them to see that there is a good reason for them to change their position and that this is something which you have conceded in other negotiations for this reason.

If you are planning to make a particular concession it is useful to see how it is likely to be received by, for example, using the 'what if . . .?' type of question. Earlier it was suggested that reciprocity was a common feature of the negotiating process. If you make a concession, you should expect to receive one back from the other side. Equally, if they make a concession, you should expect to make one yourself. You can encourage this by phrasing your concession hypothetically: 'If my client does "X" will your client do "Y", or what will your client do?'.

8.10 SUMMARY

In this chapter you have been presented with a series of related techniques designed to assist you to persuade the other side to your point of view. The importance of establishing a good rapport, the use of skilful questioning, active listening, persuasive discussion, the benefits of using an assertive style and the value of being aware of non-verbal communications have all been emphasised for their contribution to the art of persuasion. Some possible approaches to the resolution of deadlock have been suggested and finally, ways to persuade the other side to make concessions and accept yours without you losing face have been proposed. Understanding these techniques and practising them whenever you can will help you to negotiate with confidence.

Chapter Nine

Teams

In the more complex commercial deals, it is common to find that the negotiation will be conducted by a team of lawyers acting for each side. Team negotiations require a rather different approach than do one to one negotiations. Team negotiations are very complicated creatures and require a great deal of planning if they are to be effective. Where the deal is a very complex one, separate teams will be likely to be negotiating the terms of different aspects of the agreement. There is a wealth of literature on the right personality profiles required to make a team an effective one. Likewise much has been written about how teams should be managed and what communication channels should be followed to ensure that the team members are kept in touch with what is happening and are properly co-ordinated. A number of these points are dealt with in this chapter.

One cautionary word: sometimes you will be negotiating with your client alongside you; in these circumstances treat the session as though it were a team negotiation. If your client wants you there purely and simply to provide the legal technical backup, that is precisely what you should do, leaving your client to deal with the other matters wherein his/her expertise lies. Plan and agree what is to happen in advance of the meeting, in that way, you will not cross wires.

9.1 SELECTING THE TEAM

It is best to ensure that the members of the team are those likely to be best at negotiating. The members of the team should be those who have a personal reputation as good negotiators, who have experience in negotiating the particular issues which will arise in the negotiation, who have the right hierarchical status in relation to the importance of the deal and who have all, or at least many, of the skills and qualities identified in chapter 1 as likely to be present in an effective negotiator.

9.2 INDIVIDUAL'S ROLES WITHIN THE TEAM

Each member of the team will have a different role and will have different interests as well. Each member will have his/her own area of responsibility, point of view, priorities and different degrees of willingness to take risks. Sometimes the members of the team will have to spend some time negotiating between themselves so as to have an agreed strategy for the meeting.

R. M. Belbin in *Management Teams: Why they Succeed or Fail*, has argued that it is useful to have people in a team who possess strengths or characteristics which serve a need without duplicating those already there. He says that what is needed is individuals who balance well with one another because this will ensure that human frailties can be underpinned and strengths used to full advantage. Belbin identifies eight roles which team members should be willing to carry out in order for the team to be well-balanced. These are:

(a)   the company worker (the one who turns plans into action);

(b)   the chairman (the one who co-ordinates and facilitates and brings the best out of other people);

(c)   the shaper (the one who is a major force for carrying out tasks and who motivates);

(d)   the plant (the one who has the most creative ideas in the group);

(e)   the resource investigator (the one who liaises within and outside the group);

(f)   the monitor evaluator (the one who analyses and evaluates ideas);

(g)   the team worker (the one who smooths potentially disruptive influences); and

(h)   the complete finisher (the one who shows how ideas work out in detail and ensures that nothing is left out of account).

Belbin does not suggest that teams will only be effective if they have eight members, but that these skills aspects all need to be covered in some way within the group, perhaps by members taking on more than one role, in order to ensure that the team takes account of every angle.

At the negotiation itself it will not be necessary for all the members of the team to take part and it is common to find at the negotiating table only a leader or chief spokesperson, a note taker and occasionally, an observer. There are many who would advise that there is considerable value in having an observer present. It has been suggested several times that negotiations are very wearing because there is so much to take in and synthesise as the negotiation proceeds; an observer can take in perhaps more of the non-verbal clues and feed those back to the person leading the team.

If your client is with you, ensure that you have agreed roles before the meeting starts.

9.3   PREPARING THE TEAM FOR THE MEETING

It will often be helpful to prepare for any negotiation by brainstorming (see chapter 12 on preparation) with someone else what the likely issues will be and the best way to tackle them. When negotiating in a team this is absolutely essential. Each member of the group must be party to the decisions on how the negotiation is to be taken. Strategy and tactics must be agreed, as must the order and form in which concessions will be made.

9.4 AT THE NEGOTIATION MEETING

Members of the team fielded at the negotiation should only be those who are there to negotiate. Do not swell the team by taking along people who are there only to advise the negotiators.

9.5 SUMMARY

In the early stages of your career you will often find yourself working in a team negotiation. This chapter should help you to understand what your role in the team is and, as you grow in experience, suggest issues you should take into account when deciding on who should be a party to your team.

Chapter Ten

Culture and its Impact on Negotiations

10.1 INTRODUCTION

Everyone will have his or her own particular and individual style of negotiating. It is also important to recognise that people from different ethno-cultural backgrounds may have different ways of going about the process of negotiation.

It is therefore important to understand the cultural differences which can influence the success of negotiations conducted abroad, or with lawyers and business people from other countries. It is all too easy for misunderstandings to occur if differences in culture are ignored. The most important advice that can be given to anyone who is about to embark on negotiations involving those from other cultures is to spend some time identifying cultural differences and how they are likely to impact on the negotiations. Culture has been defined (by Bennett and Kassarjian in 1972, quoted in C. Leeds, *The Socio-Cultural Aspects of Anglo/French Negotiations*, 1989) as 'a set of learned beliefs, values, attitudes, habits and forms of behaviour that are shared by a society and transmitted from generation to generation within that society'. Another way of describing culture is that it exists 'when a group of people share the same ideas, tend to adopt the same behaviour and social patterns and have the same heritage in terms of accomplishments'.

10.2   CULTURAL DIFFERENCES — SOME BROAD POINTS

Leeds has suggested that the following cultural differences exist between Americans, British, other Europeans and others. The Americans, British, Germans and Swiss all seem to prefer dealing with one issue at a time; whereas the French are happy to deal either with one item or many items at the same time. Americans, British and Northern Europeans in general prefer to have a great deal of detailed information about the issues they are negotiating and rely on verbal messages to enhance their understanding of the issues involved. By comparison the French, Spanish and people from the Middle East and Japan tend to be comfortable with much less detailed information and will attach much more importance to what is not said and to non-verbal messages in order to understand the context.

When it comes to the preliminary phase of a negotiation, the pleasantries and the history of a situation, Americans tend to spend little time on this as they are generally much more orientated towards the future and the British may spend perhaps five minutes on this. Africans, Iranians, Indians and Japanese are very much more interested in the history of a matter and would want to know as much as possible about the person involved in the negotiation and so will spend quite some time on this phase of the negotiation. As to formality, Americans tend to be fairly informal and will automatically use first names. The British generally are also fairly informal, whereas the French tend to be formal and the Germans very formal. The Japanese, Chinese and Latin Americans are also very formal. When it comes to time-keeping, Americans tend to be very prompt and the British just a few minutes late; Northern Europeans, Germans and Swiss tend to be on time, the French seem to adopt the same approach as the British and are usually no more than three to four mintues late, whereas the Italians may often be about fifteen minutes late and Latin Americans, Southern Europeans and Africans tend to see time as a very flexible feature.

There are also differences apparent in the way in which different cultural groups decide whether or not to commit themselves to a negotiated deal. Americans tend to leave the ultimate decision to the person in charge. The French are more comfortable with the idea of delegating decision making, although they will occasionally adopt a more 'American approach' when they want to take more time. In contrast in Japan, China, Africa and to a lesser degree, Latin America there is much more concern to ensure that there is consensus in the group and so decisions take much longer.

In ordinary verbal communication, the British tend to wait until the previous speaker has finished what he or she has to say before intervening and will then pause before launching into a response, whereas the French are quite comfortable interrupting and finishing off what the first speaker has started to say. The British tend to control meetings very well, focusing on getting things done, whereas the French will treat a meeting in a much more relaxed and informal way. The British do not like to say 'no' and will try to find ways of avoiding saying 'no' whilst implying it. The French do not mind saying 'no' and will use 'no' without perhaps always meaning it. The British will shake hands perhaps at a first meeting and perhaps at the end of a deal as a mark of its conclusion, whereas the French shake hands as an ordinary part of day to day contact with others. The British attach great importance to the actual words used by people whereas the French give much more importance to non-verbal communication and gestures. For the British, the agreement is seen as important of itself and so the preference is to cover every eventuality within it. The French by contrast will see the agreement as more an implicit one, specifying principles but allowing for variation and further developments should conditions change. The British tend to reason in an inductive way based on facts and knowledge, whereas the French are much more likely to use deductive reasoning on the basis of concepts and general rules.

10.3   NEGOTIATING WITH THE JAPANESE

As far as the Japanese are concerned, the key message to British lawyers negotiating with them is to ensure that their approach is appropriate and that sufficient time is dedicated to the process. It is crucial to understand Japanese culture and the way that it impacts on the negotiation process or any business relationship. The time taken to negotiate an agreement by the Japanese is very much longer than would be the case in Britain. The extreme slowness of the Japanese process means that the non-Japanese negotiator should try as far as possible to slow down his or her response to the negotiation process, recognising that each area will need to be explored thoroughly and will be connected into the package as a whole, with a number of different groups. For a detailed discussion of these issues see R. I. Akroyed, *Five Blossoms: Negotiation with Japanese Business*.)

The Japanese tend to use the negotiation process and the social opportunities surrounding it as a means of filling out and checking their picture of the person they are negotiating with. The Japanese will not be comfortable following the process normally used in Britain in negotiations. So, instead of following a pattern which passes through a series of phases: opening, discussion, bidding, bargaining, closing and follow up, it is far more likely that the Japanese will begin with a preliminary meeting, and that thereafter a series of meetings will follow at which issues will be discussed and re-discussed and only gradually will the negotiators move on to bargaining, and then more bargaining. Informal, social meetings will be used to maintain the relationship between the parties. Whilst this process proceeds, these contacts are particularly aimed at ensuring that there is a real understanding and inter-personal harmony between the parties. Negotiators should recognise that negotiations on substantive points will take place both during normal working hours and during social occasions held in the evenings. Social occasions are used to build up inter-personal relationships in a more relaxed atmosphere. A harmonious climate of empathy is crucial to your potential success.

In general, the Japanese much prefer informal, often verbal argeements, to detailed written contracts. This is because by the time the agreement has been reached, there will be true and full understanding on all issues and it is therefore considered unnecessary to commit the whole thing to writing.

It is this need for mutual balance that distinguishes Japanese negotiators from non-Japanese negotiators. It will only be when they feel on the same wavelength with you that they will begin to do business with you. Everything that precedes this stage is aimed at achieving an inter-personal harmony (G. Kennedy, *Everything is Negotiable*). Early meetings are really characterised by interrogation rather than dialogue. The Japanese prefer not to do business with people who fail to treat them with respect. The Japanese like to get to know people with whom they intend to do business and they like to deal with the same people over and over again, so in selecting your team, one of the points you should always have in mind is that you field the same people. Recognising the signals that tell you what the Japanese negotiator is thinking is even more essential. It is important to be exceptionally polite, completely relaxed about your time and know that you must never take 'yes' for an answer!

10.4   HOW SHOULD YOU PREPARE FOR CROSS-CULTURAL NEGOTIATIONS?

When you are preparing for such negotiations you should:

(a)   ask yourself whether those from the culture with whom you will be negotiating are likely to display a preference for a different style of negotiation from that which you would normally adopt;

(b)   ask yourself whether the usual strategy that you would adopt, in the particular context of the negotiation, is appropriate given those cultural differences;

(c)   think about the things that you may misinterpret;

(d)   research if you can whether there are other strategies that are commonly adopted in the culture with which you will be negotiating, and what their component parts are; and

(e)   try to discover whether there are any ethical considerations which you should bear in mind.

When it comes to opening the negotiations, things to consider are whether you should get straight to the point, what kind of atmosphere would help and what format you should use for your opening statement. When it comes to the discussion part you need to think about whether the usual methods you adopt to persuade people to your point of view will be appropriate or not, and the extent to which your listening skills and questioning skills need to be adapted to meet the cultural norms of the person with whom you will be negotiating. In relation to bargaining, you need to think about the nature of the concessions you will make, and the form of the concessionary style which is the norm for the country with which you are dealing. You also need to think about the tactics which are appropriate and seen as acceptable. Also think about issues related to stress. The impact of deadlines is particularly important, find out whether the other side will always need to go back to get approval for what they have negotiated before it becomes final. Finally consider the actual format which the agreement will take.

Chapter Eleven

Alternative Dispute Resolution

No account of the nature of negotiations between lawyers would be complete without some reference to alternative dispute resolution techniques (ADR). These techniques were developed in the United States of America in the 1970s and have gradually been introduced in the United Kingdom, initially in the form of conciliation procedures in matrimonial cases and employment cases. These techniques are now gathering momentum as providing particularly helpful ways of solving commercial disputes fairly, effectively and efficiently.

ADR is a system of dispute resolution which avoids the need for public proceedings in a court of law. It is not simply an alternative to proceedings, but can also be used alongside on-going litigation. Its aim is to achieve the best possible commercial solution to a problem by enabling the parties to be as creative as they like in finding a way to solve their difficulties. Finding the appropriate solution will depend on what the parties' interests are, looking at the past, their current business relationship and at their future commercial or other objectives.

There are a number of potential advantages to be gained by participating in ADR:

    (a)   It enables a business or other solution to a problem to be found which meets the particular needs of the parties without jeopardising any of their legal rights through having participated in the process.

(b)   It is an entirely private process and so negative publicity is avoided.

(c)   Business and personal relationships are likely to be better sustained because the need for allegation and cross allegation is avoided. The process looks to the future rather than the past.

There are a number of techniques available to parties seeking an ADR solution. These include the mini-trial (the executive tribunal), mediation, neutral fact finding, neutral experts and private judging. The most commonly used forms are the mini-trial and mediation.

In the context of this book I shall concentrate solely upon mediation as a form of negotiation. Mediation is assisted negotiation. A successful outcome is achieved through the involvement of a third party whose primary role is to assist the parties to negotiate effectively. One of the attractions of the system is that mediation is said to offer a risk free means to learn more about the situation and about the other side's point of view. Indeed, Fisher and Ury recommend mediation as a way of breaking deadlock reached in a negotiation although mediation is just as useful when used as a formal means of negotiating.

11.1   THE ROLE OF THE MEDIATOR

The neutral third party mediator persuades the parties to focus on their underlying interests and concerns and to move away from the fixed positions that often obscure the real issue. The mediator operates as a 'facilitator' who has no personal stake in the dispute, but who does have a personal stake in helping the parties to achieve a settlement. The mediator assists communication by clarifying the parties' interests, by helping to build on the existing relationship between the parties and by trying to defuse antagonisms by, if necessary, knocking heads together if obstinacy appears to be keeping the parties apart.

The essence of the mediator's task is neatly summarised as:

> A mediator holds joint and separate meetings with those in
> conflict in order to reduce hostility and establish effective
> communication, assist people to understand each other's needs
> and concerns, ask questions which reveal the real interests of
> each side, raise and clarify issues overlooked or inadequately
> covered, assist people to develop and communicate new ideas,
> help re-frame proposals in more palatable terms, moderate
> unrealistic demands, test receptiveness to new proposals, help
> craft agreements which solve current problems, safeguard
> relationships and anticipate further needs. (Andrew Floyer
> Acland, *A Sudden Outbreak of Common Sense: Managing
> Conflict Through Mediation*.)

The role of the mediator is generally to defuse tension and
aggression. Mediators need to have some understanding of why
people behave in the way that they do and be able to listen actively
and empathise. They enable both sides to define and clarify their
positions and objectives as they listen to and disentangle a mixture
of fact, emotion, prejudice, perception, assumption and opinion.
Mediators need to be able to think creatively. Mediators have to
work to build trust, have to be able to use their personality, convey
human warmth, sympathy and have a sense of humour. Mediators
have to be professionals in the sense of having absolute integrity,
being impartial at all times and trained.

11.2   HOW DOES MEDIATION WORK?

The mediator is in effect using a problem solving or principled
negotiating strategy to help the parties find a solution to their
difficulty. (See chapter 3 on negotiation strategies.) Mediators will
be trying to make a negotiation move towards a problem solving
strategy, whatever form of strategy the parties have previously used
and whatever the nature of the dispute.

There are two different types of mediation — 'facilitative' and
'evaluative'. Where the facilitative form is used, the mediator does
no more than help the parties communicate with each other so that
they can reach agreement. In these cases the mediator acts largely to

defuse anger and frustration and divert confrontation. Where evaluative mediation is used, the mediator learns the facts of the case, each party's views and each party's position, and then expresses to each party a view on the overall merits as he or she sees them.

Because a mediator does not have a direct interest in the outcome of the mediation, the mediator is more likely to be able to establish the truth underlying each party's position and be able to direct the parties towards the parameters within which agreement could be reached. Mediators are able more easily to introduce criteria for objectively arriving at one possible solution by giving an external and objective view of the fairness of solutions proposed by each side. Mediators may well be able to bring the parties together by forging an agreement that both takes account of common interest and finds ways around any differences between the parties.

It can be seen therefore that mediation offers many advantages as a system, but it must also be recognised that to be a successful mediator within that system calls for the deployment of the fullest range of negotiating skills used at the highest professional level.

Chapter Twelve

Preparation

Taking the time to prepare properly is a necessity not a luxury. Careful and thoughtful preparation will mean that you are properly equipped to enter into a negotiation. In a negotiation, there is always a risk that the other side will surprise you in some way. The more carefully you have prepared the groundwork, the less likely it will be that the other side will be able to surprise you.

A failure to prepare adequately will become apparent very quickly both to the other side and also to your own client. You will find it difficult to respond adequately to any proposals that might be made; and you might find yourself agreeing to something on which you have no instructions or worse still, on which you do have clear instructions but not to do what you have just agreed to do! If your client accompanies you to the negotiation meeting, the impression you will create, if you are not well prepared, will not augur well for a continuing relationship with that client.

As you gain experience as a negotiator, you should aim to create a series of checklists which will help you to develop set patterns which you will eventually be able to use in any negotiation. In this way much of the hard work involved in preparation will become so automatic that you will not need to spend quite so much time at this, the preparation stage. Some basic checklists are provided for you to use at the end of this chapter.

Adequate preparations for negotiation involve several elements amongst which are included the following topics.

12.1 KNOWING THE FILE

Although it seems rather obvious, before seeking to negotiate, you must be on top of the file. You will occasionally see senior practitioners picking up a file at the last minute and rushing off to a meeting without having a full understanding of, or having forgotten, what they should be seeking to achieve. Avoid this approach — suggestions about personal management are made in Stephen Mayson's book in this series, *Personal Management Skills*, which should help you to use your time well enough to ensure that this situation does not arise. Time spent in effective preparation is never wasted.

Whilst reviewing the information contained in the file, you should particularly concentrate on the information you will need during the negotiation itself. Always take the opportunity to remind yourself of all the facts as you understand them from your client and from the other side. Review the evidence and the whole history of the matter. This will help to ensure that you cannot be taken by surprise by the other side. You will know exactly what has been agreed so far and which issues appear to be sticking points. Checking the information held on file will also help to ensure that you know your client's instructions and what your client's objectives are.

Understanding who wants the deal or wants to settle the litigation the most will help you to understand and use the power interplay beween the parties. You will then be able both to advise your client realistically and prepare yourself mentally to recognise who is likely to gain the upper hand in the negotiation and to identify which issues are most likely to have to be conceded.

It is always useful to identify issues as of either major or minor importance, both from your client's point of view and from the other side's point of view, and where these issues are likely to interact with each other. This will enable you to work out how to trade issues, one for another.

In litigation, understanding both the strengths and weaknesses in your evidence will enable you to identify those matters where you will be able to push home the advantage and those you need to play down so as to enable you to take as realistic an approach as possible to the conduct of the settlement meeting.

You will be looking to make the best use possible of the facts which are most likely to be in your client's favour. Remember though, the facts which are likely to be favourable to your client may not exactly mirror those which you identify as the other side's weaknesses.

Identify what information the other side needs to know. Prepare a list of the factual matters you will need to explain to them. Keep the list as short as you can and, if possible, reduce the list to a number of main headings. (See chapter 5 on the process and chapter 8 on persuasion.)

12.2   KNOWING THE LAW

Whether you are negotiating the terms of an agreement or to settle a case that will otherwise go to court, you must be sure of the law which will determine such issues as: what warranties should be included in the contract; what measure of damages should apply if any warranties are broken; what the basis for liability will be; and what the likely measure of damages will be if the matter goes to court.

You must be sure of your ground in the sense of being up to date with statute law including statutory instruments, and with case law, as well as with the typical lines of arguments which are likely to be used. You will need to know what the average agreement of the type you are negotiating usually looks like, which clauses will be included and in what form. Understand the authorities which will support your contentions but also ensure that you know what authorities the other side is likely to rely on and what, if any, arguments there are which could be raised against them.

To take, as a specific example, a commercial agreement for the sale and purchase of the shares in a company which provides for the ordinary common law measure of damages for breach. You are likely to have to work hard to have a clause included which also entitles your client to the indemnity basis of damages. To have any chance of succeeding in this, you will need to understand what the legal consequences of your requirements are likely to be for the other side and think of ways to justify to them the additional risks involved. Think of all the reasons why, from your client's point of view, this appears to be a fair and reasonable arrangement and list down your points. Your list might well look something like this:

COMMON LAW MEASURE AND INDEMNITY BASIS OF DAMAGES

Common law measure leads to problems in trying to access market value if both measures used can concentrate on establishing whether the breach occurred or not.

Indemnity avoids time consuming arguments that shares may not be worth what was paid.

Can be fairer since avoids arguments that the shares are worth what was paid for them even though there has clearly been, for example, an understatement of liabilities.

12.3 UNDERSTANDING YOUR CLIENT'S INSTRUCTIONS AND OBJECTIVES

Unless you know what your client wants to achieve and how far your client is willing to go in order to achieve his or her objectives, you will not be properly prepared and able to take part in a negotiation fully confident of your purpose and the needs of the client. Particular problems can arise if you have failed to follow this simple rule.

Imagine being in the middle of a negotiation meeting with things moving along at a pace in the direction which serves your client's interests best, when suddenly the other side presses you for a completion date, in effect wanting to know when your client will be able to come across with the money. You know that the price is right as you have your instructions on this but if you have failed to establish exactly when your client wants to, or will be able to complete the deal you will lose credibility. You would have to leave the meeting in order to take your client's further instructions causing everyone to waste time. Worse still would be the need to check your instructions with your client if your client is with you at the meeting. You certainly would not want your client to interrupt proceedings so as to call a halt. You will lose face both with the other side and with your own client if this happens. There are also the costs to bear in mind. Market research has clearly shown, particularly in recessionary times, that clients will be happy to pay what they believe to be a fair price for the deal that they want, but that they will not be happy to pay when they feel that you have failed to conduct the matter efficiently and effectively, especially if this results in the whole process being unnecessarily extended.

Again, in litigation, it is just as important to establish what your client's ultimate objective is. It may be the desire to have their day in court, if so that is what they must have and you must clearly warn them of the financial consequences of this, especially if, in the end result, they lose. Alternatively, following your advice on the law, the facts and the likely remedy, they may, for example, have a figure in mind at which they would be willing to settle. You must establish in advance what that figure is or the range within which they would be willing to settle. Never forget the impact which costs (both your's and the other side's) will have and so ensure that this element has been considered by your client and is taken into account when a decision about quantum is made. In some cases the whole purpose of the litigation may be to delay paying for something which your clients know they will have to pay for in the end. In such cases careful calculations will be needed to establish the time at which it is financially appropriate to concede or partially concede. Other clients may want to squeeze the last penny from the other side and so will not settle until they reach the door of the court. The moral is, know what your client wants, and having advised your client on your understanding of what is achievable within the legal realities, carry those instructions through.

You also need to have established what the client's view is of a failure to agree. A client may see reaching an agreement as desirable but not an absolute necessity. They may have wholly different objectives in mind, for example they may want to stall and not rush into an agreement until perhaps another transaction has been completed, or they may just want to obtain as much information as possible from the other side before deciding whether or not to press ahead with the negotiations. You should establish what their 'best alternative to a negotiated agreement' is (the client's 'BATNA' as it is called by Fisher and Ury in *Getting to Yes: Negotiating Agreement Without Giving In*; see 3.3). What are the alternatives?

On every issue you will need to establish: what the ideal solution is from your client's point of view; what your opening position should be (the further this is from the ideal solution the greater your room for manoeuvre); what would be a satisfactory solution (that is, one which will be acceptable to your client even if not the ideal); and finally, what the bottom line is. The bottom line is the absolute minimum which the client is prepared to accept. Careful agreement on each of these levels will ensure that you know the parameters of your authority.

What if the other side has the stronger bargaining position, how can you prepare so as to protect yourself? The relative strength of each party's bargaining position in the negotiation depends primarily on how attractive to each is the option of not reaching agreement. In many cases negotiators will seek to protect themselves by having a bottom line because this makes it easier to resist pressure in the heat of the moment and can make clear for you precisely what your client has authorised you to do. If you are playing in a team all the team members will then know what the parameters are. Fisher and Ury argue that a BATNA is better than having a bottom line (see chapter 3 on negotiation strategies).

Whilst working out your own BATNA it is also important to think about what the BATNA will be for the other side and if they over-estimate their BATNA you will want to lower their expectations. It can be particularly useful for you to have a good BATNA against a powerful other side.

12.4 KNOWING THE OTHER SIDE'S CASE AND OBJECTIVES

Another crucial element in obtaining a successful outcome to a negotiation, because you will then have a better understanding of which issues to pursue and which to minimise in importance, is to know as much as possible about the other side's case. What do you think they want? What have they told you they want? For example, if they are desperate to do the deal because they need the money it will provide to fund other parts of their business or to service their bank loans, your client will probably have the upper hand in terms of bargaining power. Alternatively, if there is a lot of competition to do the deal, there will be less room for manoeuvre especially if your client is very keen to do the deal.

How can you find out this kind of information? Start by checking out these kinds of issue with your client. Also check the press, particularly the financial press for any information which may give you a clue to the other side's situation or motives, and use whatever information retrieval systems you can to learn about the other side's needs. It is just as important for you to know whether the other side is in no hurry or indeed is in two minds about whether this particular deal will benefit them or not, because you will need to think about ways to coax them to go ahead. You will then need to think carefully about the aspects of the deal which will seem the most appealing to the other side.

In litigation, the motives of the other side are often the most difficult issues to work out. There are those who, whatever the costs, will want to have their day in court, and with these kinds of opponent there is not a lot you can do to dissuade them from that course. For many though, the extremely high cost of litigating a matter to a court decision will encourage them to settle, even if it is at the door of the court (for example, some 99% of personal injury cases will settle in this way). Clearly the greatest encouragement to settlement is the hugely escalating cost of the action as it proceeds towards trial.

Try to work out what your opponent is seeking to achieve: for example, if damages are being claimed as the remedy, know what the range of damages is likely to be, know what the costs will be, including those which will probably not be paid by the loser; try to establish whether the real aim of the litigation is to delay payment; always keep an eye on the financial soundness of the other side; ask your client whether the parties will need/want to maintain a relationship (be it a working relationship, or in a divorce case a relationship because there are children of the family) once the action ends; consider whether alternative dispute resolution techniques might appeal (see chapter 11 on alternative dispute resolutions).

Throughout you will be seeking to establish the motives of your opponent, the strength of their case and what they want out of the whole thing. Consider the possible solutions to their needs, including those which are not available as remedies which a court could order. They can help you to achieve a settlement.

Finally, identify those aspects of the other side's needs that will help you to understand the basis of their claim. You can list a number of issues about which you will want to ask questions particularly during the discussion phase (see chapter 5 on the process) so that progress can be made at the negotiation meeting. Identifying more precisely their needs will help you to look for ways of maintaining mutual advantage for both sides.

Your preparation may lead you to believe that there are some objectives which are common to both sides. Know what these common objectives are so that you can use them early in the meeting to encourage the belief that the negotiation can be a success for both sides.

Note that the weaknesses which you identify in the other side's case may not be the same as the strengths you have identified in your own case.

12.5 KNOWING THE OTHER SIDE

Find out whether anyone else in your firm has negotiated with the other side before. Try to get a feel for the personality and style of the person you are likely to face across the table. This information will help you to know what approach to take and what style you should adopt for the meeting. Look on all negotiation meetings you attend, whether as notetaker or as a more senior member of the team, as a way of gathering data. You are likely to come across the same people again. You may also find that some firms have a particular style when negotiating — the more you learn about the people you may meet on the other side the better prepared you will be.

12.6   EXPANDING THE CAKE

Part of your preparation should be to look at the problem which the negotiation is intended to resolve from the point of view of expanding the ways in which your client's objectives can best be met. Gather a long list of ideas about optional solutions to the problems. It is often best to brainstorm with a group of others who understand the problem you are trying to solve and so, if you are negotiating in a team (see chapter 9 on teams), this is one of the activities in which the whole team can take a part. There are certain ground rules which must be followed in brainstorming, the most important of which is the no criticism rule. What is important is to gather in as many ideas as possible, so the group should be encouraged to throw in ideas whether they appear sensible or not. It is only when all the ideas have been collected that you will set about identifying those which appear to be the most promising and then try to improve them.

If you are in the process of litigating a matter, then thinking widely about the objectives of your client should mean that you can think how to resolve the issues between the parties in ways which might not be possible remedies available from a court. The recent development of the structured settlement provides an excellent example of creative thinking aimed at helping both sides. The structured settlement looks at the options and seeks to satisfy both sides' objectives; the plaintiff's objectives being to be assured of financial security which, for the severely injured, could be for life; and from the defendant's point of view, to find the most cost effective means of achieving this.

In negotiating the terms of a sale of goods or services contract, the parties may be willing to accept, in return for a lower price, less responsibility for liability should something go wrong in the performance of the contract. In share sale and purchase agreements, it may be possible to trade agreement to a higher price in return for a continuing and guaranteed market from the seller for the goods being produced, for a given period of time, at an agreed price. The range of possibilities is endless, what matters is that you have thought about the possibilities as creatively as possible bearing in mind, where appropriate, the commercial needs of your clients. A brainstorming session with the client aimed at unmasking all these possibilities can be particularly helpful.

12.7 PREPARING YOURSELF

Having immersed yourself in the detailed preparatory work stand back and then begin again by reflecting on the purpose of the negotiation and what you hope to be able to achieve. Think about how you expect to get what you want and how long it is likely to take. Think about how you want to present information to the other side, what you want to tell them and also what you want to learn about the other side's needs. Think about the strategy you should adopt, understand what the strengths and weaknesses of your case and the other side's case are or are likely to be; think about the issues from both the point of view of negotiating a resolution and from failing to reach agreement. Know where the bargaining strength lies, know both who is in the weaker position in general and in respect of each and every issue which will fall to be discussed during the negotiation. Decide which negotiating strategy to use and which tactics to use.

If you are thinking of using a problem solving strategy (see chapter 3 on negotiation strategies), you should identify the objectively fair standards which you will want to use to enhance the appeal of your suggestions aimed at solving the problem and reaching agreement. Criteria which can be relied upon here include:

(a)   in a negotiation about price, market value;

(b)   in a negotiation about terms or quantum, be it damages, salary, pension rights, or a similar issue, consider using an approach based on precedent;

(c)   in a negotiation relating to how a contract will be performed, professional or industry norms can be useful;

(d)   in a negotiation aimed at solving problems that would otherwise have to be litigated, what a court would decide;

(e)   in almost any negotiation, evidence tending to establish that the proposed result will be the most efficient, that the alternatives will increase costs, and an appeal to morality can all be effective.

Reliance can be placed on expert opinion to set the standard; or if you can establish that there is a traditional way of dealing with something you can rely on that tradition. Thus, in a commercial contract for the sale of a business the tradition is that the buyer drafts the agreement. You can appeal to the other side to act reciprocally; or you can rely on that most commonly used, objective fair standard, 'split the difference'.

Prepare yourself for the bidding phase of the negotiation, work out what bids you will make in relation to each and every issue or aspect of the negotiation. Identify those issues where your client is willing for you to make concessions and those where no concession should be made. Identify those concessions which will cost your client very little but which may be particularly valuable to the other side. Prepare your opening statement and practise it (see chapter 5 on the process).

If you are working in a team, think carefully about how you will carry out your allotted role (see chapter 9 on teams). If you are negotiating with lawyers from overseas, find out all you can about their particular cultural system and its likely impact on the negotiations (see chapter 10 on culture and its impact on negotiations).

With practice you should be able to develop an opening statement, the bones of which can be used every time you enter into a negotiation. Once you have been able to do this you will gain confidence from knowing exactly how you are going to begin and not having to fumble for words (see chapter 8 on persuasion).

12.8 PREPARING THE AGENDA AND FOR THE MEETING

If possible always try to set the agenda for the negotiation meeting. The agenda should include the various points which you want to discuss and your preferred order for discussing them. Think particularly about the difficult issues and the most appropriate point to raise them. Often it will be best to sprinkle them about, but much will depend on the strategy you have decided to adopt. You may feel that it will be best to concede all the points you are willing to concede first, and place the more difficult ones at the end, but beware of this as a general tactic (see chapter 4 on tactics). You will then have more control of the issues which are to be considered and the order in which they are to be raised.

Although there may be conventions about where the negotiation meeting is to be held, if you have drafted the documents, it generally makes more sense for you to hold the meeting at your offices. In any event you should feel more comfortable about holding the meeting at your own premises (see chapter 5 on the process and chapter 8 on persuasion).

You must consider who should attend the meeting. Should your client be there? Will it be better to keep your client in reserve so that final approval of the agreement, and what has been conceded to obtain it, can be approved outside of the meeting? (See chapter 4 on tactics.)

How long do you want the negotiation meeting to last? Do you want to give it only a limited time, perhaps to keep the discussion short, or are you happy to keep going for as long as will be necessary to do the deal? (See chapter 7 on psychological aspects.)

12.9 SUMMARY

Preparation is one of the most important parts of the whole negotiation process and so you must do everything that you can to be on top of your own case — what is the history, what are the facts, what are the legal points you can use to support your position, what does the client want to achieve, what are the issues which are the most important, what are the issues that are least important, what are the client's instructions on each of these? If possible develop a range of solutions to the problem, and identify which your client prefers, i.e., make the cake as large as possible.

Know as much about the other side's position as you possibly can — why do they want to contract, or to litigate, what facts are they relying on, what do they appear to be emphasising most, what legal arguments are they likely to rely on, how might their cake be enlarged, what kind of people are they, what negotiating style are they likely to adopt?

Prepare your agenda. Check that you have instructions on every point which is to be raised at the meeting. Go to the meeting, and good luck!

12.10 PREPARATION CHECKLISTS

12.10.1 The file and client information

(a) Who approached whom?

(b) Why does your client want to do the deal?

(c) Why does the other side want to do the deal?

(d) Who wants to do the deal the most?

(e) If your client wants to do the deal the most, why is this?

(f) If the other side wants to do the deal the most, why is this?

(g) From your client's view point, what elements of the deal are the most important?

(h) From your client's view point, what elements of the deal are likely to be the most difficult to achieve?

(i) From the other side's view point, what elements of the deal are likely to be the most important?

(j)   From the other side's view point, what elements of the deal are likely to be the most difficult to achieve?

(k)   Will the parties continue to have a relationship once the deal has been done?

(l)   What are the strengths and weaknesses of your client's case?

(m)   What are the strengths and weaknesses of the other side's case?

(n)   Have there been previous transactions between the parties — what is the history of them?

(o)   Has there been an exchange of Heads of Agreement or a Letter of Intent ? If so, what has been suggested in either of those documents?

(p)   What points can be conceded?

(q)   What points cannot be conceded?

(r)   Who else has dealt with the other side before?

(s)   What kind of person and negotiating style does the other side use?

(t)   Do the parties have a shared interest in preserving their relationship?

(u)   What opportunities will there be in the future for continued co-operation?

(v)   What would it cost to break off negotiations?

(w)   Are there any common principles like a fair price that both sides can accept?

12.10.2   Your personal style, strategy and tactics

(a)   How do I behave under pressure?

(b)   What do I know about how the other side behaves under pressure?

(c)   What makes me angry?

(d)   What do I know about what makes the other side angry?

(e)   How do I react to anger?

(f)   What do I know about how the other side reacts to anger?

(g)   How do I feel and behave when I am frustrated?

(h)   What do I know about how the other side behaves when frustrated?

(i)   What are the warning signs that I am beginning to behave irrationally?

(j)   What do I know about the warning signs that the other side is beginning to behave irrationally?

(k)   How quickly do I recover after making an emotional outburst?

(l)   What do I know about how quickly the other side recovers from emotional behaviour?

(m)   Is there anything in my approach to the problem which may upset the other side?

(n)   Do I expect anything in their approach to the problem to upset me?

(o)   What strategy shall I adopt for this negotiation?

(p)   What strategy do I expect the other side will use in this negotiation?

(q)   What tactics shall I use to:

    (i)   carry out my chosen strategy?

    (ii)   change their choice of strategy?

    (iii)   deal with the other side?

    (iv)   satisfy my client?

    (v)   maintain my reputation?

    (vi)   meet the time constraints?

(r)   What tactics do I expect the other side to use to:

    (i)   carry out their strategy?

    (ii)   change my choice of strategy?

    (iii)   deal with me?

    (iv)   satisfy their client?

    (v)   maintain their reputation?

    (vi)   meet the time constraints?

Bibliography

A. Acland, *A Sudden Outbreak of Common Sense: Managing Conflict Through Mediation* (Business Books, 1990).

R. I. Akroyed, *Five Blossoms: Negotiation with Japanese Business* (University of Nottingham, 1989).

G. Atkinson, *The Effective Negotiator: A Practical Guide to the Strategies and Tactics of Conflict Bargaining* (Negotiating Systems Publications, 1983)

R. M. Belbin, *Management Teams: Why They Succeed or Fail* (Heinemann, 1981).

R. Fisher and S. Brown, *Getting Together: Building a Relationship that gets to Yes* (Business Books Ltd., 1989).

R. Fisher and W. Ury, *Getting to Yes: Negotiating Agreement Without Giving In* (Business Books, 1989).

P. Gould and R. Gould, *From 'No' to 'Yes': the Constructive Route to Agreement* (Video Arts, 1988).

O. Hargie (Ed.), *A Handbook of Communication Skills* (Croom Helm, 1986).

L. Hawkins, M. Hudson and R. Cornall, *The Legal Negotiator: A Handbook for Managing Legal Negotiations More Effectively* (Longman Professional, 1991).

V. Helps, *Negotiating: Everybody Wins* (BBC Books, 1992).

D. M. Hosking and I. E. Morley, *A Social Psychology of Organising: People, Processes and Contexts* (Harvester Wheatsheaf, 1991).

G. Kennedy, *Everything is Negotiable* (Business Books Ltd., 1990).

A. King, *Effective Communication* (Blackstone Press, 1992).

C. Leeds, *The Socio-Cultural Aspects of Anglo/French Negotiation* (University of Nottingham, 1989).

A. Pannett, *Managing the Law Firm* (Blackstone Press, 1992).

S. Le Poole, *Never Take No For An Answer: A Guide to Successful Negotiation* (Kogan Page, 1991).

D. G. Pruitt, *Negotiation Behaviour* (Academic Press, 1982).

B. Scott, *Negotiating Constructive and Competitive Negotiation* (Paradigm, 1988).

R. Sharpe, *Assert Yourself: How to Do a Good Deal Better with Others* (Kogan Page, 1989).

S. Soderberg and W. Scott, *The Art of Managing* (Gower, 1985).

H. Twist, *Effective Interviewing* (Blackstone Press, 1992).

J. White, *The Pros and Cons of Getting to Yes* (1984) 34 Journal of Legal Education 115-16.

G. Williams, *Legal Negotiation and Settlement* (West Publishing, 1983).